THE
WOMEN
OF
THE TALMUD

THE
WOMEN
OF
THE TALMUD

Judith Z. Abrams

JASON ARONSON INC.
Northvale, New Jersey
London

The author gratefully acknowledges permission to quote from the following sources:

From *The Midrash on Proverbs*, translated from the Hebrew with an introduction and annotations by Burton L. Visotzky. Copyright © 1992 by Yale University Press. Used by permission of the publisher, Yale University Press.

From *The Tosefta*, edited and translated from the Hebrew by Jacob Neusner. Copyright © 1977, 1979, 1981, 1986 by Jacob Neusner. Used by permission of Ktav Publishing House.

This book was set in 12 pt. Korinna by Alpha Graphics of Pittsfield, New Hampshire, and printed by Haddon Craftsmen in Scranton, Pennsylvania.

Library of Congress Cataloging-in-Publication Data

Abrams, Judith Z.
    The women of the Talmud / Judith Z. Abrams.
      p. cm.
    Includes bibliographical references and index.
    ISBN 1-56821-283-6
    1. Women in rabbinical literature. I. Title.
  BM509.W7A25   1995
  296.1'2'0082—dc20   94-22410

Manufactured in the United States of America. Jason Aronson Inc. offers books and cassettes. For information and catalog write to Jason Aronson Inc., 230 Livingston Street, Northvale, New Jersey 07647.

"A joyful mother of children" (Psalm 113:9)

For Hannah, Ruth, and Michael

Contents

Preface
and Acknowledgments

When I was in my first year of rabbinical school in Jerusalem I was trying my hardest to learn Hebrew. So every *Shabbat* I would attend services at a synagogue in my neighborhood, *Ohel Aharon*, in Rehavia. It was, naturally, an Orthodox synagogue and to enter it I had to walk all the way around the back of the *shul* and climb some stairs to reach the balcony. From there, I could look down as the men led the service and I tried to follow along as best I could.

Did this segregation bother me? Not really, because I had a secret joy that I knew the men did not share and did not even know existed. Each week, when we came to the hymn *Lechah Dodi* in which we welcome *Shabbat*, we would all turn toward the entrance to greet *Shabbat* as if greeting a bride. I knew that down there, on the main floor, all they saw if they looked out the windows or through the door was the apartment building across the street. But when I looked out the window from the balcony, I looked over the apartment buildings and each week I saw a magnificent sunset over Jerusalem. This was a view the men were never vouchsafed and it came to be one of the most precious parts of my Sabbath celebration.

I hope that this book can serve as a window on another precious world, a world that has been overlooked for some time. Our rabbinic literature records the actions of many women, most of them never named, who can inspire men and women today with their courage, independence, and thirst for learning and life. I made the acquaintance of these women, so to speak, first by simply stumbling across them in the course of working on my Ph.D. dissertation, and then by actively seeking them out in the literature. By bringing some of this material together into one volume, hopefully women will see that they have ancestors who were just like them: searching for a Jewish life and seeking to control that life as much as possible.

I am grateful to God for the opportunity to write this book. In addition, I am grateful to Arthur Kurzweil, Marion Cino, Pamela Roth, and Janet Warner of Jason Aronson Inc. for giving me the opportunity to write it and helping me to do so. The following persons read the manuscript and provided me with many helpful suggestions: Dr. David Kraemer, Ms. Jeanie Krim, Dr. Ava Miedzinski, and Rabbi Joseph Radinsky. In addition, Dr. Judith Hauptman and the Beth Yeshurun Library in Houston, Texas, helped me by providing background materials. Of course, I am most grateful to my husband, Steven, and our children, Michael, Ruth, and Hannah, for allowing me to complete this work.

Introduction

The Task at Hand

Imagine what a historian, fifteen hundred years from now, would think about women's everyday lives today if all that she had to study were women's magazines. Or perhaps the historian could recover only rock videos or legal records. Would the historian ever be able to grasp what an average woman's life was like in our day and age? If we could talk to that historian we might say, "Well, wait a minute! Some women's lives resemble your historical artifacts, but certainly not all women's, and even regarding the women you find in your records, this is only one small part of their existence! Women are a complex, varied group of individuals: poor and rich, gifted and dull, beautiful and ugly, righteous and evil. You can't lump them all together and say this is what a woman's life was like!" "But I want to know *something*," answers the his-

torian, "and this is all I have to go on." We might then
answer, "All right, go ahead and write what you wish, only
remember that you write on the basis of limited evidence
and don't make too many generalizations. Nonetheless,
you may get *something* of a feel for what it was like to
be a woman in the twenty-first century." As an extra bit
of help, we might suggest that the historian look at the
women of his or her own day and draw analogies from
their natures to ours. In this study, we will take the role of
the historian and I imagine that, were we able to speak
with the women of the rabbinic era whose lives we will
attempt to describe, they might say to us precisely what
we would say to that historian in 3500.

What do we have to go on as we try to discover what a
Jewish woman's life was really like in the rabbinic era
(70 C.E.–500 C.E.)? We have inscriptions that concern
women and these have already been explored in Bernadette J. Brooten's book *Women Leaders in the Ancient
Synagogue.*[1] We also have the record of a group of people
—the sages who wrote rabbinic literature—to provide us
with an answer. Surely if women had written their own history, it would have been quite different from the accounts
we find in rabbinic literature. Nonetheless, rabbinic literature is what we have in hand and we do want to know something about what a Jewish woman's life was like fifteen
hundred years ago. So we will examine the way women
are portrayed as *behaving* in that literature. Note well,
we are not going to examine what the sages thought about
women, or what they thought women ought to do in theory.
Much has been written on these topics (see the Bibliography), but that is not what interests us here. Rather, we
are going to examine those episodes, recorded in rabbinic
literature, that claim to recount what women actually *did*.

When we look at these materials we will find that women were every bit as varied a group then as women are now: some were pious and respectful of the sages, some didn't think much of them; some were poor and others rich; some longed to be married while others suffered the unwanted proposals of men or yearned for a divorce. What may most greatly surprise us as we study these materials is the large amount of power and control women had over their own lives. They were far from the passive, powerless figures we might have thought them to be.

The Nature of Our Sources

We will examine three sorts of materials from rabbinic literature that describe the ways women behaved in this era: (1) case law and case histories involving women whose stories reflect, possibly better than any other material in rabbinic literature, the nature of women's lives, (2) tales about women, often the sages' mothers, wives, sisters, slaves, daughters, and granddaughters and, (3) materials and stories about women whose characters are well-outlined in rabinic literature and about whom we have a relatively generous amount of material.

The first sort of material is probably the most credible in terms of telling us how women really lived. Case histories and instances of case law are where the sages' ideas intersected with the real world. These cases appear to be part of a body of precedents that were evidently known to those who composed rabbinic literature and that were brought to support or refute points under discussion. Therefore, it seems likely that these cases actually happened. We may regard as particularly credible those instances of case law that could have involved a person of either gender (e.g., cases regarding property law). If the sages were to make up such a case it seems unlikely that they would make up a case about a woman. It is more likely that they would generate such a case history about a man. Therefore, when we come across a case that could have involved either a man or a woman, and it does concern a woman, we may consider that that case has a higher likelihood of actually having happened than any of our other material. How do we find these cases? These passages all include the key phrase, "a certain woman," and are included either in a list of case law developed by Jacob Neusner[2] or are simply part of rabbinic literature.

The tales we will examine are distinguished from the case histories by the fact that they are (1) shaped literarily (e.g., the story has symmetry and balance), (2) they illustrate a text from the *Tanakh*, the Jewish Bible, and/or (3) they contain some aspect of the supernatural. While examples of case law are often portrayed as taking place in court or when an individual consults a sage, tales have a wide variety of venues. We must consider these tales skeptically when gathering data about women's lives. Though these stories may contain a kernel of historical truth they are usually greatly embellished and therefore the material in them is suspect as historical data.

The stories about well-known women have many of the characteristics of tales. Such tales in rabbinic literature, whether about men or women, are not considered by today's scholars to accurately portray ancient reality. Nonetheless, they do tell us about certain persons' images within the sages' community. While we may not take them as fact, they can still tell us how certain women came to be seen by the sages.

The Sages' Agenda and Our Own

First, last, and always we must remember that the materials we have were included in rabbinic literature because the sages *wanted* them to be included. They serve to illustrate points that the sages chose. Therefore, to understand these materials we must understand how they fit into the sages' agenda. The sages recognized in women both the universal and the specifically female.

The sages saw that women were simply human beings whose natures transcended gender, whose beings were part of the universal human condition. As such, women could study Torah and have their learning be as valued as men's. In principle, the sages believed that power, whether in personal relationships or in society at large, stemmed from virtue and, this being the case, women could wield power as easily as men. The sages also recognized that women experienced and perceived truth and that their testimony could be important in serving the pursuit of truth in court. Thus, with some ambivalence, they allowed women to testify in court even when other rabbinic teachings would appear to disqualify them from giving testimony. In other words, women were human beings and when they, or their life stories, validated the sages' value system, their deeds were seen as valuable and powerful and were recorded for posterity.

On the other hand, the sages saw that some things were part of women's lives alone and men had little, if any, input into these areas. Naturally, these areas concerned women's distinctive physical nature and ascribed role in society. The sages related to the processes of menstruation, pregnancy, birth, and lactation in two ways. First, the sages could serve as authority figures; helping to legislate practice with regard to these issues, functioning almost as diagnosticians in some ways. For example, they would determine whether a given vaginal discharge was unclean or not. However, the sages seemed to have recognized that these were experiences that were distinctly female and allowed women to legislate much of the behavior related to the processes of menses and childbirth for themselves. The sages also responded to the mysteriously foreign processes of women's bodies in symbolic ways, seeing in women the embodiment of life and death; the embodiment of ambivalence itself. When the sages respond to women in this way, we can see that they may have envied the power evident in women's bodily processes.

In this book we will follow a woman through her life cycle as a Jew, beginning with her study of Torah, which forms the basis of every Jewish life. We will also explore the particular case of the matron and possible precursors to today's women's Torah study groups. Next, we will examine how women entered and exited relationships. This chapter will also allow us to contrast the way the sages thought about women (as recorded in the *Mishnah*) and the way women actually behaved at these moments of transition (as reported in the *Gemara*). Being able to differentiate between theoretical statements in rabbinic literature and reportage of case histories is one of the most important tools in dealing with the anger many women (and men) feel as they read this literature. When we come across a sexist statement in rabbinic literature, if we are able to look at its context and say, "Oh, that's just a theoretical statement and people were not bound by it then, and they aren't now," we are then able to read the text with a great deal more comfort. Most people, at least most women, who study rabbinic literature, go through a phase during which they become angry at the sexism in what they read. Part of the agenda of this chapter is to offer the reader tools that can help him or her move beyond this phase of relating to the literature. Next, we will examine the way women wielded power in their relationships and in the world at large. We will also look at the way women's testimony was validated by the sages. The next chapter deals with women's behavior during menses, sexual intercourse, and childbirth, and the final chapter shows how some women coped with death and loss.

At every turn we will see women who defy conventional wisdom (both of the sages' era and our own) about a woman's role in the Jewish world. We will find that while some women were undoubtedly unlearned, passive, powerless, and oppressed, many other women were learned, powerful, and willing and able to manipulate people and Jewish law in order to make their lives better. In each chapter, we will relate Jewish women's lives then to Jewish women's lives now. In other words, today's Jewish women who study and who lobby for (and seize) greater power in the Jewish community are not orphans but the spiritual children of those ancient women who did the same and who can serve as role models for their spiritual progeny today.

The Five Major Works of Rabbinic Literature

As we examine our sources, we must be mindful of their contexts. Rabbinic literature is made up of five major works, each of which has its own characteristic traits.

Because we draw on all five sources of material in this volume, a brief introduction to each of them is in order. The five main works are (1) the *Mishnah*, (2) the *Tosefta*, (3) the Talmud of the Land of Israel (the *Yerushalmi*), (4) the *Midrash* collections and, (5) the Talmud of Babylonia (the *Bavli*). Those parts of the Talmuds that are commentary on the *Mishnah* are called *Gemara*. The term *Talmud* refers to the *Mishnah* and *Gemara* combined.

Rabbinic literature is frequently called the Oral Torah. Tradition has it that God whispered the laws and customs contained in the Oral Torah to Moses on Mount Sinai at the same time God gave Moses the Written Torah (the first five books of the Bible). This Oral Torah was passed down through the generations, "from Moses to Joshua; Joshua to the elders; the elders to the prophets" (M. *Pirkei Avot* 1:1). Many scholars believe that the teachings of the Oral Torah developed during a much later period. Regardless of the time of its genesis, the Oral Torah was the sages' method of making the Written Torah meaningful to the people of their day. The following is a brief table summarizing some important historical information about the different works of rabbinic literature and the abbreviations we will use, with the name of the tractates, or individual books of the Oral Torah, to identify this material.

	Date Finished	Place Finished	Abbreviation
Mishnah	200 C.E.	The Land of Israel	M.+ tractate name
Tosefta	220–230 C.E.	The Land of Israel	T.+ tractate name
Yerushalmi	400 C.E.	The Land of Israel	Y.+ tractate name
Midrash	400–500 C.E.	The Land of Israel	full name used
Bavli	427–520 C.E.	Babylonia	B.+ tractate name

These Five Works as "People"

How do these five different kinds of rabbinic literature differ from one another? In general, the *Mishnah*, which was compiled first, contains an outline of how the law given in the Written Torah is to be followed. It is more theoretical than practical. Practical details are provided by the *Tosefta*, *Yerushalmi*, and the *Bavli*. The *Midrash* collections are unique in that they are made up principally of stories that expound biblical passages rather than focusing primarily on Jewish law and practice.

One way to understand the interrelationship of these rabbinic writings is to think about them as different personality types. *Mishnah* is like a dreamer who is always imagining how things should be rather than thinking about how they are. This sort of person is always concocting beautiful schemes to organize her life. The only problem is that these dreams don't necessarily relate to reality.

Tosefta is like the *Mishnah*'s more practical friend. When the *Mishnah* goes off on an idealistic tangent, *Tosefta* says, "Wait a minute. I don't think that's going to work the way you think it's going to. And what if conditions change? And have you thought of all the consequences?"

The *Yerushalmi* is like *Tosefta*, only more so. The *Yerushalmi* listens to the *Mishnah* and *Tosefta* and then takes over the conversation, citing statistics and information from a vast library of knowledge. The *Yerushalmi* may take a long time to come to a decision, but usually it will eventually tell you that, "Yes, the *Mishnah*'s plan will work" or "No, the *Mishnah*'s plan won't work, but *Tosefta*'s might" or "Neither the *Mishnah* nor the *Tosefta* have it right. However, I have an answer I've dug up that I think *will* work."

The *Midrash* collections, which comment on different books of the Bible rather than on the *Mishnah*, as does the rest of rabbinic literature, are loners. They're loosely connected to the *Mishnah*, *Tosefta*, and *Yerushalmi* and *Bavli*, but they really go their own way. They're like that one member of a circle of friends who is included but not terribly attached. And are they into telling stories! The difference between the *Mishnah* and the *Midrash* collections is that the *Mishnah* wants to pretend that her dreams are going to shape reality. The *Midrash* collections want to tell stories and find meaning and enjoyment in life without necessarily legislating that vision. It's sort of like the difference between a politician (the *Mishnah*) and a political commentator (the *Midrash* collections): one is into prescribing solutions and the other is into talking about problems and brainstorming ideas.

Finally, the *Bavli* is like the *Yerushalmi* . . . and not like the *Yerushalmi*. Like the *Yerushalmi*, the *Bavli* listens to the *Mishnah* and *Tosefta* and then takes over the conversation. However, unlike the *Yerushalmi*, the *Bavli* isn't so "bottom line" oriented. The *Bavli* is more interested in exploring options than in determining the one right solution to a problem. Also, the *Bavli* loves to tell stories; almost as much as the *Midrash* collections do. Finally, the *Bavli* is a bit more talkative than the *Yerushalmi*—who was already quite talkative.

If you ever gathered these five "people" in a room, the *Mishnah* would start the conversation, next *Tosefta* would get in a few comments, then the conversation would be taken over by the *Yerushalmi* and the *Bavli*. The *Midrash* collections would be over in a corner studying Torah and occasionally contributing to the conversation.

Because of the nature of the materials we are studying, we will rarely trace a subject through all five documents. We will not find our material gathered together but rather spread throughout rabbinic literature. Therefore, we will have to consider the case histories and tales within their individual contexts and then, looking at them together, try to discern patterns that might hint at what women's lives were like in the rabbinic era.

Some Notes on Style and Translations

A few words should be said about the style used in this book. Indented passages are selections from the *Tanakh* (the Jewish Bible) or rabbinic literature. *Bavli* passages are cited according to their traditional folio numbers from the Vilna edition and passages from the *Yerushalmi* are cited according to the Venice edition. When a passage is found in more than one place within rabbinic literature, these parallel passages will be noted with the symbol "//" plus the name of the work and the page number on which it appears. The word *Mishnah* with a capital M indicates the entire work: all six tractates. The word mishnah with a lower case "m" indicates one small passage from that work.

The translations of rabbinic literature used in this book are adapted from Jacob Neusner's translations of *Tosefta* and the *Yerushalmi*, the Soncino translation of *Midrash Rabbah*, Burton L. Visotzky's translation of *Midrash on Proverbs*, Reuven Hammer's translation of *Sifre on Deu-*

teronomy, and the Soncino translation of the Babylonian Talmud, edited by Maurice Simon. Although gender-inclusive language is used in the text, the translations reflect that the language used to describe God in rabbinic literature is most often in the male gender.

One final caution must be provided. We can never definitively prove what women's lives were like fifteen hundred years ago. All we can do is examine the evidence and hopefully make our interpretation of it seem more likely to be correct than some other interpretation of it. As Erwin Goodenough notes, "Such a book, like all historical reconstruction, should properly be written in the subjunctive mood: what I say *may* be the case. It would be so written except that the subjective mood is rhetorically tiresome."[3] I have tried to follow Goodenough's example and to make clear the tentativeness of the conclusions reached herein without becoming "rhetorically tiresome."

1

Torah Transcends Gender: Women and Sages' Learning

A woman colleague tells the story of a man who adamantly refused to have her perform his father's funeral. "A rabbi must have a beard!" he railed at her. She calmly explained to him that no other rabbi was available and that his only choices were to have her perform the funeral or to have no funeral at all. Eventually, she did officiate at the funeral in her usual caring and professional manner. After the service was over, the man reportedly approached her and said apologetically, "You grew a beard."

This story embodies a basic truth that the sages of rabbinic literature recognized: Torah learning transcends gender. The sages were able to recognize and value wisdom and learning in persons regardless of their gender. While women may not have had as many opportunities to study Torah as men, when they did have access to Torah study and were engaged in transmitting it, their learning was as valued as men's was. Conversely, women could, like men, be ignorant of Torah and in need of enlightenment. As in every age, and with regard to every gender, some individuals treasured Torah and some did not, and the case histories and stories that are preserved in rabbinic literature give us glimpses of both sorts of women: the learned and the ignorant.

Beruriah's Law

Any consideration of women expert in Jewish law and lore in the rabbinic era must begin with Beruriah. She was the daughter and wife of sages. Her father, Hananya ben Teradion, was a teacher in the second century C.E. in the Galilee (B. *Sanhedrin* 32b). Only a few of his teachings (M. *Pirkei Avot* 3:2, T. *Mikvaot* 6:3, B. *Menachot* 54a) have come down to us. Beruriah married Rabbi Meir, an extremely important sage whose teachings shaped the *Mishnah* as we have it today. From those materials that are preserved in Beruriah's name, we can discern a clever intellectual who was able to find solutions to intricate problems as well as able to develop explanations of biblical verses and use them in ingenious ways.

Let us first examine the two halakhic (Jewish legal) pronouncements ascribed to Beruriah. Both pertain to a specific item's ability to become ritually impure. Whether something can become impure relates, in part, to its fitting into a cultural category. Generally, the item must be a whole, recognizable item in order to have ritual impurity adhere to it.

We can understand this in the following way. Imagine that you are sitting in a kitchen and someone asks you to identify everything in the room. You will name the objects that have cultural significance to you: the stove, oven, refrigerator, cans of food, and so forth. You will likely name whole, working objects first. Now let's say that there is a crumpled cellophane wrapper sitting in a cabinet. The person asking you to identify things in your kitchen will ask, "What's that?" and you might well say, "Oh, that's nothing." The wrapper is incomplete, psychologically and culturally insignificant, when it is not wrapped around a box.

Beruriah's rulings help to identify the exact moment when an item moves from the category of "complete item," in which it can receive uncleanness, to the category "incomplete item," in which it cannot become ritually impure.

> When does it [a certain kind of oven] become clean? . . .
> R. Halafta of Kefar Hananya said, "I asked Simeon ben Hananya, who asked the son of R. Hananya ben Teradion, and he said, 'When one will have moved it from its place.' And his daughter says, 'When he will have removed its garment.'" When these things were reported before R. Judah b. Baba, he said, "Better did his daughter rule than his own son." (T. *Keilim Bava Kamma* 4:17)

The item under discussion here is a small, round oven that is covered with plaster. Something, let's say a mouse, has entered the oven and died there, making the oven impure. The question is, "What is the minimum amount of disassembling of the oven that we must do until it no longer fits the cultural category 'oven'?" We don't want to disassemble it more than we have to (think about your own oven and this becomes clear). The best solution will be the one that requires the least damage to the oven so we may put it back in working order as quickly as possible and with as little expense as possible. The suggestions in the *Mishnah* (M. *Keilim* 5:7) range from cutting it into pieces to moving the pieces about. It is this opinion that Hananya ben Teradion's son appears to be echoing.

Beruriah suggests a less disruptive solution: one need only remove the mud coating on the oven to render it no longer culturally recognizable as an oven. (Again, think of a modern analogy. Whose opinion would you rather follow: the one that will make you take your oven out of the wall and break it into parts and reassemble it or the one that simply tells you to take the door off your oven? Either way, the oven is no longer functional, but one involves a great deal more grief than the other.) When R. Judah ben Baba hears of Beruriah's decision he applauds it: hers is the least disruptive decision that still achieves its goal of rendering the oven nonfunctional.

Such ovens and their cleanness or uncleanness caused many a conflict, perhaps the most famous being the one between Rabbi Eliezer and the sages found in B. *Bava Metsia* 59a–b. Rabbi Eliezer declared such an oven clean if it were cut into parts and sand put between the parts, but the sages declared it unclean. Rabbi Eliezer held so firmly to his view that he was excommunicated. A picture of such an oven is provided in Adin Steinsaltz's translations of *Tractate Bava Metsia*.[1]

Beruriah's other ruling is quite similar. At issue is the identity of a part of a door bolt and the sages' difficulty in placing it in a category. The passage discusses the part of the door bolt that is used to slide the bolt across the door. It is a large peg with a rounded top that is used as a handle to move the bolt. (A picture of this peg can be found in Adin Steinsaltz's Hebrew translation of *Tractate Eruvin*.[2]) Apparently people would take this peg out of the door bolt and use it to grind spices as with a mortar and pestle. So is it an item unto itself (in which case it can always become unclean)? Or is it simply a part of the door bolt, that is, not a whole item unto itself (in which case it is not susceptible to uncleanness)? There is great puzzlement on this issue (for example, in M. *Eruvin* 10:10 and M. *Keilim* 11:4): the sages were in conflict about what category this item fit into. The issue is resolved in *Tosefta*:

> A door bolt—R. Tarfon declares unclean and the sages declare clean. And Beruriah says, "One removes it from this door and hangs it on another on the Sabbath." When [these] rulings were reported before R. Judah, he said, "Beautifully did Beruriah rule." (T. *Keilim Bava Metsia* 1:6)

The majority of sages (whose opinions are generally taken to be the law) suggest that the door bolt, even if it might be used as a pestle, is clean, that is, it is not an item unto itself. However, there is some conflict about this. So what does Beruriah suggest? She suggests that we take it from one door and hang it on another door on *Shabbat*. This way it is surely clean since it does not work except in the door it was made for. Why? A modern analogy may help. A key may always be a cultural item, recognizable on the face of it. But it is only "real" when it is in the lock it is designed for. If you put a car key in your front door lock, it is clear that the key is not accomplishing anything. Beruriah's solution makes the logic of the sages' decision clear: the door bolt (the "key") is only a whole item when it is used in the bolt it was designed for. And just as one may use a key to accomplish tasks besides opening doors (e.g., one can use a key to open cans of pop) they are not the real purposes for which the key was created and so may be considered culturally insignificant. And why does Beruriah suggest that the bolt be transferred on *Shabbat*? To indicate decisively that it is not a whole item and may be moved on the Sabbath; something that is ordinarily prohibited for whole items (e.g., a lock and a key or the door bolt and the door together). R. Judah comments once more on Beruriah's cleverness: she is able to make fine distinctions and use her intellect.

Beruriah's Lore

Beruriah was not only an expert in questions of *halakhah* but in the area of biblical studies as well. In this passage, we find some evidence of discrimination against Jews from Lod, in the south of Israel, and those from Nehardea in Babylonia. Y. *Pesachim* 5:3 explains that the discrimination is based on the prejudice that those from the south of Israel and Babylonia are too full of pride and do not study Torah enough. (Such regional chauvinism still operates today. For example, when interviewing for jobs in Texas, rabbis from other parts of the country invariably wonder if they will have a congregation full of cowboys.) A scholar from these ancient locations is compared unfavorably with Beruriah.

Rabbi Simlai came before Rabbi Jochanan [and] said to him, "Let the Master teach me the Book of Genealogies [a commentary on Chronicles]." Said he to him, From whence are you? He replied, From Lod. And where is your dwelling? In Nehardea. Said he to him, We do not discuss it, either with the Lodians or with the Nehardeans, and how much more so with you, who are from Lod and live in Nehardea! But he urged him, and he consented. Let us learn it in three months, he proposed. [Thereupon] he took a clod and threw it at him, saying, Beruriah, wife of Rabbi Meir [and] daughter of Rabbi Hananya ben Teradion, who studied three hundred laws from three hundred teachers in [one] day could nevertheless not do her duty in three years, yet you propose [to do it] in three months! (B. *Pesachim* 62b)

Here, it would seem, is an elaborate put-down of Rabbi Simlai. He comes from places that make it inappropriate for him to learn this commentary on the Book of Chronicles and he proposes to do it in an inappropriately quick way, reinforcing the stereotype about sages from Nehardea being too proud and not studying Torah appropriately. As part of this denigration, Rabbi Simlai is compared unfavorably with Beruriah, who apparently ordinarily learned intensely and quickly, yet could not complete studying this commentary in three years.

Perhaps the most interesting thing about this passage is that the phrase "do her duty" is the translation of *yatstah y'dei hovatah*, "she fulfilled her obligation," a technical phrase usually applied to those who are obligated to perform a *mitsvah*, a commandment. Here, it is applied to Beruriah. This would seem to imply that whoever composed this story felt that Beruriah was obligated to study this commentary to Chronicles just as a man would be. Usually, women are not considered obligated to study Torah (that is not to say that it is not praiseworthy, just that they are not *obligated* to do so), yet here we find that Beruriah *is* considered obligated for at least one specific act of Torah study.

A Woman Studies Weekly

Were some women considered obligated to study Torah? Did some women pursue Torah study aggressively? Another passage suggests that this may have been a more common phenomenon than we have been led to believe. Evidently, women could attend synagogue to pursue their studies. In the following story, we find that a woman faithfully attends lectures by Rabbi Meir and this causes some strife with her husband, who apparently does not attend the lectures. While this is clearly a legend, it was evidently considered credible by those composing the tale that a woman would regularly attend synagogue in order to study. This story is part of tractate *Sotah*, which is concerned with the ritual whereby a woman suspected of adultery drinks water into which a text containing God's name has been ground.

> Rabi Meir would teach a lesson in the synagogue of Hammata every Sabbath night. There was a woman who would come regularly to hear him. One time the lesson lasted a longer time than usual. She went home and found that the light had gone out. Her husband said to her, "Where have you been?" She replied, "I was listening to the lesson." He said to her, "May God do such and so and even more if this woman enters my house before she goes and spits in the face of that sage who gave the lesson." Rabbi Meir perceived with the help of the Holy Spirit [what had happened] and he pretended to have a pain in his eye. He said, "Any woman who knows how to recite a charm over an eye—let her come and heal mine." The woman's neighbors said to her, "Lo, your time to go back home has come. Pretend to be a charmer and go spit in his [Rabbi Meir's] eye." She came to him. He said to her,

"Do you know how to heal a sore eye through making a charm?" She became frightened and said to him, "No." He said to her, "Do they not spit into it seven times, and it is good for it?" After she had spit in his eye, he said to her, "Go and tell your husband that you did it one time." She said to him, "And lo, I spit seven times?"

Rabbi Meir's disciples said to him, "Rabbi, in such a way do they disgracefully treat the Torah [which is yours]? If you had told us about the incident with the husband, would we not have brought him and flogged him at the stock, until he was reconciled with his wife?" He said to them, "And should the honor owing to Meir be tantamount to the honor owing to Meir's Creator? Now, if the Holy Name, which is written in holiness, Scripture has said is to be blotted out with water so as to bring peace between a man and his wife, should not the honor owing to Meir be dealt with in the same way!" (Y. *Sotah* 1:4, 16d // *Leviticus Rabbah, Tsav* 9:9)

This story forms a commentary on the practice of *sotah*, the trial by ordeal that a wife suspected of adultery had to undergo, as well as on the importance of the marital bond. The ritual of the bitter waters (*sotah*) is detailed in Numbers 5:11–31. A suspected adulteress was made to drink special water into which a passage containing God's name, among other things, had been added. If she came to no harm from it, she was deemed innocent. If she was guilty, her belly would swell. The main point of our passage from the *Yerushalmi* is this: marital harmony is so important that God allows the Holy Name to be blotted out in this water in order to clear a wife's honor. Therefore, a sage's honor should likewise be sacrificed to this all-important goal. There seems to be some difficulty with the text. The commentary P'nei Moshe on this passage in the *Yerushalmi* suggests that the text might better be read: She should tell her husband that she spit in Rabbi Meir's eye seven times, thus far exceeding her husband's demand that she show disrespect to this great teacher by spitting in his eye once. (This is the version of the text that appears in *Leviticus Rabbah, Tsav* 9:9.) We note with interest that it is Rabbi Meir, Beruriah's husband, who is teaching this woman and helping her. Could it be that Rabbi Meir was exceptionally open to women studying Torah? This passage suggests that this may have been the case.

What is important for our study is that it *was* plausible that a woman would faithfully attend lectures by a great rabbi in a synagogue and that the woman's aim in coming to the synagogue was to learn. It is also telling that this causes marital strife, whereas tales of men's studying causing such strife are relatively rare. This does not mean that some women did not resent the time their husbands spent in study, simply that their complaints were not preserved. This seems a bit like the way the content of magazine articles is skewed today: there are more articles about women feeling guilty about leaving their children to go to work than about men feeling that way. This is not to say that men do not have these feelings, simply that the culture affirms one group's feelings more strongly than another's.

It is safe to say that whenever there is a large difference in the level of Jewish commitment between marriage partners it will become a source of conflict between the spouses regardless of the gender of the partner who is most committed. Indeed, very religious persons who marry "secular" Jews find themselves marginalized in their communities. For example, their *frum* friends might not eat in their homes for fear that the nonobservant spouse does not observe the laws of *kashrut*. And imagine the conflict that could be engendered when a woman wants to observe the laws of *niddah*, which involve abstaining from sex for part of each month, and her husband does not. This is an "equal opportunity" source of conflict: either male or female partner can be the one who is more serious about Judaism. The solution is "equal opportunity" as well: good communication, an ability to compromise, and a knack for living with diversity.

Rabbi's Maid: An Unexpected Expert

Even a woman who had little in the way of a formal Jewish education could be an expert in some areas. For example, Rabbi's maid was apparently a bit of an expert in Hebrew. Rabbi is Rabbi Judah Hanasi, who composed the *Mishnah* around the year 200 c.e. He was an extremely prominent sage and, interestingly enough, many stories about his housekeeper have been preserved for us and will be examined at different points throughout this volume. Here, Rabbi's maid teaches the sages who gather at Rabbi's house.

> The rabbis did not know what was meant by *serugin* [till one day] they heard the maidservant of Rabbi's household, on seeing the rabbis enter at intervals, say to them, How long are you going to come in by *serugin*?
> The rabbis did not know what was meant by *haluglugot* till one day they heard the handmaid of the household of Rabbi, on seeing a man peeling portulaks, say to

him, How long will you be peeling your *haluglugot*?
(B. *Rosh Hashanah* 26b //B. *Megillah* 18a)

Why did Rabbi's maid know these Hebrew words and the sages did not? An answer suggested by the late Professor Jakob J. Petuchowski was that the upper classes had, by this point in history, come to use Aramaic, which was the lingua franca of the period, as their language, while the lower classes continued to use the older Hebrew language. It was in this everyday language that obscure Hebrew words and their meanings were preserved. It is something like the use of the Creole language in Cajun country. The "upper classes" who attend universities speak standard English while those who stay on the bayous and islands continue to speak the Creole language.

One of the most impressive things about this story is that the sages listen to the everyday speech of this maid. Today, sadly, we tend to treat janitors, maids, sanitation workers, and the like as invisible, as having nothing to teach us. At least in the case of Rabbi's maid, the sages did not succumb to this trap: they treated her with respect, listened to her words, and believed they could learn from her as well as from her illustrious employer.

Whether it was the technical, halakhic knowledge of Beruriah, the study of Torah offered by Rabbi Meir and partaken of by the anonymous woman in our legend, or women's "folk knowledge" of Hebrew, women were obviously recognized as learned. And just as some women today are more Jewishly knowledgeable and some less, so we find that some women in the sages' era were enamored of Jewish learning and some were not. It is to these less-learned women that we now turn our attention.

Women Who Did Not Keep Kosher

There seems to be a tendency in human nature to glorify the past and denigrate the present. Thus, we may look back to our grandparents' generation as the one that had true Judaism. We are not alone in this tendency. The last *mishnah* of M. *Sotah* consists of a long list of the merits of past generations as opposed to present ones. So, for example, we learn the following:

> When Rabbi Meir died, the makers of parables were no more. When Ben Azzai died, there were no more industrious scholars. When Ben Zoma died, there were no more expositors [of biblical texts]. When Rabbi Joshua died, goodness ceased to exist in the world. (M. *Sotah* 9:15)

This listing goes on for quite some time in a similar fashion. While this practice shows a healthy and pious tendency to honor our ancestors, we should not confuse it with accurate historical reporting. In fact, we have some evidence in our sources to suggest that ignorance of the *mitsvot* and assimilation were serious problems in the sages' era, just as they are today. For example, we find that observance of the laws of *kashrut* may not have been universally rigorous in the sages' days.

> Rav once happened to be at Tatlefush and overheard a woman saying to her neighbor, How much milk is required for cooking a quantity of meat? Said he [Rav], do they not know that meat cooked with milk is forbidden? He [therefore] stayed there [some time] and declared the udder forbidden to them. (B. *Chullin* 110a)

The sages prohibited meat and milk from being cooked together. So Rav was quite distressed to hear two women calmly discussing a recipe for an ancient version of beef stroganoff and took this as an opportunity to acquaint the community with the laws of *kashrut*. This story is brought to illustrate M. *Chullin* 8:3, which mandates that the udder of an animal must be cut open and the milk therein drained out before it can be cooked as meat. Apparently Rav was concerned that the people of Tatlefush would not observe such a fine point of law and thought it prudent to "make a fence around the Torah" and simply forbid them to cook and eat the udder and thereby keep them from possibly mixing the meat of the udder with the milk that it contained. It might be similar today to a rabbi walking into a congregation and hearing the brotherhood plan a breakfast menu with ham in it. The rabbi would probably take the opportunity to educate his or her brotherhood about the laws of *kashrut* and might say, "Cook dairy only," just to be on the safe side.

Women Who Intermarried

We tend to view the problems of intermarriage and lax observance of Judaism as unique problems of our era. While these problems are certainly grave today, we are by no means the only generation to experience them.

> Rabbi Chiyya bar Abba once came to Gavla, where he observed Jewish women who conceived from proselytes who were circumcised but had not performed the required ritual ablution; and he saw that idolaters were mixing Jewish wine and Israelites were drinking it, and he saw

that idolaters were cooking lupins and Israelites ate them; but he did not speak to them on the matter at all. He came before Rabbi Jochanan. He [Rabbi Jochanan] said to him: Go and announce that their children are bastards; that their wine is forbidden as *nesek* wine; that their lupins are forbidden as food cooked by idolaters, because they are ignorant of the Torah. (B. *Yevamot* 46a)

Here is a whole town full of Jewish women who are married to men who are somewhere between gentile and Jew. It seems that these men intended to convert but had not yet completed the process. (There was an understandable delay between circumcision and immersion in the *mikveh* in the conversion process for men since they needed time to heal. However, this period had evidently been overextended in this case since these men were healed enough to have had intercourse that produced pregnancies. If they were healed enough to engage in sexual intercourse, they should have been well enough to immerse themselves in the *mikveh*.) And this was not the only "relaxed" observance of Judaism in this community. They also allowed idolaters to be in contact with their wine. Wine in this era was prepared by mixing together a thick concentrate of wine with water to dilute it to a palatable strength. Normally, idolaters were not allowed to touch Jewish wine lest they dedicate some of it to their pagan gods. Such wine, which has the taint of idolatry associated with it, is called *yen nesek* and is forbidden to Jews. In addition, for similar reasons, idolaters were not to cook Jewish food lest they set aside a portion of it for their gods. When Rabbi Jochanan hears of these practices, as did Rav in the previous case, he rules that all these actions are prohibited because he sees that this community is not learned in Torah and so would not be able to distinguish between practices that are near the edge of acceptability and those that are over the edge and not legitimate Jewish practice.

We may wonder if Rabbi Jochanan's pronouncements against this community carried any weight with the inhabitants there at all. After all, today many small, isolated Jewish communities (and some not so small or isolated) develop their own Jewish practices. Pronouncements about these practices emanating from New York or Jerusalem do not seem to carry much weight with these communities. If they feel it is legitimate Judaism, then there is little that authorities in distant places can do except discredit these communities and their practices as a whole as Rabbi Jochanan did here.

What is the solution to the problem of assimilation? Where is the balance between Rabbi Chiyya bar Abba's accommodation to such practices and Rabbi Jochanan's rejection of them? Perhaps these issues must be decided on a case-by-case basis. Regardless of the answer we develop today, it may be a comfort to us to know that this problem of assimilation has been with the Jewish people for at least fifteen hundred years and we have not capitulated to it yet.

These women were ignorant of some basic Jewish practices, as were many men in this era. Other women were knowledgeable about Judaism and their deliberations were on a par with the sages'. Women were as varied a group then as they are now. Their knowledge was valued and their ignorance condemned, just as it was for men. Torah knowledge and ignorance of Torah transcend gender, then and now.

2

The Matron:
Jew or Non-Jew?

Her Background

The "matron" is different from any of the women we will encounter in this volume. She is not one person but rather a member of a social class. Some suggest that she may be a fictional character the sages set up as a "straw Roman woman" who asks questions to which the sages may offer clever answers, thus demonstrating the superiority of Judaism and the sages' interpretations of it. When we look carefully at our sources, however, we gain a very different picture of this class of women. In our sources from the Land of Israel (the *Yerushalmi* and *Midrash* Collections) these women are portrayed as seeking Jewish knowledge. In the *Bavli*, these women are depicted as persons of influence.

We have to wonder, "Why a woman? Why not a man in these passages? What connotations were attached to

a woman's questions that were not attached to a man's?"
Rarely do these stories require that a woman be in them.
Usually, the non-Jewish questioner could equally well be
the male "philosopher" or the *min* (Judeo-Christian) who
is also a frequent theological "sparring partner" of the
sages. Interestingly, the passages in rabbinic literature that
feature the *min* are much more hostile in tone than those
that feature the matron. The *min* is often called a fool
(*shoteh*) by the sages; the matron never is. In fact, we
have to ask another basic question about the matron. All
the traditional commentaries assume that matron means
"*Roman* matron." However, as we shall see when we look
carefully at our sources, there is nothing about the matron's
questions or actions, except in one case (and even in that
case, some doubts can be raised), that are specifically
Roman. In fact, many of her actions seem much more
logical if she is Jewish. Why would a Roman woman be
asking a sage about the meaning of a Jewish text? Wouldn't
the logical woman to ask a sage about a Jewish text be a
Jewish woman?

We know that in the pagan Roman world and the Christian world during the rabbinic era, wealthy widows held
prominent positions in society and, in the case of Christianity, became important, knowledgeable supporters
of the church who achieved everything but the rank of
priest. Might the matron be the Jewish counterpart to
these knowledgeable, influential churchwomen? Might
they, like many women of today, be quite involved in the
working of the synagogue; supporting it and participating in the learning it had to offer? Indeed, it seems quite
logical that these matrons, if widows left substantial wealth
by their husbands, could well have had the luxury of free
time to devote to the pious pursuit of Jewish knowledge

and that the sages would take the time to teach these powerful supporters of their institutions. Certainly, the surrounding culture in the rabbinic era could have supported women who took such a course of action, since Christian women were doing so. Let us examine our sources with an open mind as to the nature of the matron we encounter there.

A Role Model for Dealing with Rabbinic Rejection

The following story is brought as an illustration of this famous (or infamous) mishnah:

> She has hardly finished drinking when her face turns yellow and her eyes protrude and she is covered with swollen veins. And they say, "(Take her out,) take her out, that she does not defile the Temple Court!" If she had any merit, this suspends her punishment. There is merit that suspends punishment for one year, there is merit that suspends punishment for two years, there is merit that suspends punishment for three years. From this Ben Azzai says, "A person is required to teach Torah to his daughter. For if she should drink the water, she should know that [this] merit suspends for her [the punishment]." Rabbi Eliezer says, "Whoever teaches Torah to his daughter, it is as if he teaches her lewdness." (M. *Sotah* 3:4)

Knowing the context for Ben Azzai's and Rabbi Eliezer's teachings is more important than usual in order to correctly understand the statements in this *mishnah*. If we take them out of context we would imagine that Rabbi

Eliezer thinks it is a bad thing to teach women Torah. That is not what he is conveying with his statement. This *mishnah* describes, in part, what happens when a woman suspected of adultery goes through the trial-by-ordeal of drinking bitter waters. If she is guilty and has no merit that might delay the punishment, she swells up and turns yellow. However, if she has any merit, then the punishment is delayed. Torah study is the sort of meritorious act that delays the punishment. Therefore, Ben Azzai thinks that all fathers should teach their daughters Torah so that if they must go through this ordeal they will have some merit that will delay the punishment. Rabbi Eliezer thinks the opposite: if a father teaches his daughter Torah, she will know that punishment will be delayed and she will be more likely to commit adultery, thinking she can do so and not be punished immediately. This is the meaning of their statements in context. However, as with many other statements, these came to be understood in ways that differed from their original intent. So we see that Rabbi Eliezer's teaching seems to have become a general rule about not teaching women Torah at all, in any circumstances.

> A matron asked R. Eleazar, "How is it that, though only one sin was committed in connection with the [golden] calf, those who died, died by three kinds of execution?" He said to her, "Woman has no wisdom except at the distaff, for it is written, 'And all the women that were wise-hearted did spin with their hands (Exodus 35:25).'" Said to him Hyrcanus, his son, "So as not to answer her with a single teaching from the Torah you have deprived me of three hundred *kors* of tithes per year!" He said to him, "Let the teachings of the Torah be burned, but let them not be handed over to women." (Y. *Sotah* 3:4 19a)

First, let us examine the question the matron asks for it gives evidence of an extensive knowledge of Jewish law. The sin of worshiping the golden calf would appear to be a single sin that should be punished by a single mode of execution. However, according to further material in this same passage, depending on whether those who sinned had a trial, were witnessed sinning, or were admonished against sinning, they were either executed through a court trial, through trial-by-ordeal, much like the drinking of the bitter waters by a suspected unfaithful wife, or by a plague. Alternatively, it is suggested that they may have died different deaths because they offered something to the calf, danced before it, or merely rejoiced in their hearts at the making of the calf; dying of a court trial, trial-by-ordeal, or plague, accordingly. This matron's question is an interesting one that displays a good bit of familiarity with the story of the golden calf and the laws of capital trials in Judaism. However, Rabbi Eleazar refuses to teach her anything and urges that she not ask such questions, saying that women should occupy themselves with hand work, not Torah study. Is it likely that a pagan or Christian woman would have known this much about the Jewish interpretation of the golden calf story? It seems just as, if not more, logical to assume that it was a Jewish woman who knew not only the biblical story but some of the rabbinic embellishments of it and was puzzled by the inconsistency.

Though the woman's verbal response is not recorded, we can deduce that she is put out by Rabbi Eleazar's answer from Rabbi Eleazar's son's reaction. Apparently he and his father were Levites who were the beneficiaries of tithes. Had they maintained good relations with this woman they, and not some other member of the levitical class, would receive the tithes from this woman's property. A *kor* is the equivalent of 7 bushels or 246 liters, so a good bit of material wealth was at stake in this interchange. Her ability to give so much in tithes also suggests that this matron may have been the Jewish corollary to pagan and Christian wealthy matrons. We note that it seems more logical that a Jewish woman would offer tithes rather than a pagan or Christian woman. Regardless of the economic loss involved, Rabbi Eleazar (some suggest Rabbi Eliezer, as in M. *Sotah* 3:4) holds to his teaching that women ought not to be taught Torah.

Any woman who has experienced the frustration and rage of having her interest in Torah rejected solely because she is a woman will identify with this matron immediately. Here is a person who, if she had been of the "correct" gender, would have had a future as a sage. She asks a knowledgeable, perceptive question and is slapped down with a rude retort to know her place. Who knows what she said? Clearly she took her money with her and left. Maybe she went to another sage to learn and continued to gain knowledge of the Torah from those more willing to teach her. This woman is a good role model for women attempting to enter the world of Torah study today. If one is rebuffed, one should take one's money, interest, and time and invest it all elsewhere, with someone who can appreciate these gifts, rather than continuing to try and receive satisfaction from someone who is clearly not going to provide it.

Good Relations between a Sage and Matrons

The next several passages involving a matron are portrayed as conversations with R. Yose ben Halafta. He was a sage in the mid-second century c.e. A student of Akiba, he was a highly respected and influential teacher and his court in Sepphoris was recognized as one of the most outstanding. He was influential not only in determining Jewish law but also in explicating complicated theological issues through the Torah text, as in the following passages.

In this interchange, the question a matron asks shows a great deal of knowledge of Torah on her part. To understand our next passage, we must know that Genesis 5:1–31 outlines the generations between Adam and Noah using a standard format. Almost every generation follows the paradigm we can see in these verses:

> And Seth lived a hundred and five years, and begot Enosh. And Seth lived after he begot Enosh eight hundred and seven years, and begot sons and daughters. And all the days of Seth were nine hundred and twelve years; and he died.
> And Enosh lived ninety years and begot Kenan. And Enosh lived after he begot Kenan eight hundred and fifteen years and begot sons and daughters. And all the days of Enosh were nine hundred and five years; and he died. (Genesis 5:6–11)

As we can see, this is almost a "fill in the blank" sort of format. Only the names and numbers change in the description of each generation. For this reason, the description of Enoch's generation seems quite odd.

> And Enoch lived sixty and five years, and begot Methuselah. And Enoch walked with God after he begot Methuselah three hundred years and begot sons and daughters. And all the days of Enoch were three hundred sixty and

five years. And Enoch walked with God, and he was not;
for God took him. (Genesis 5:21–24)

Enoch is described as "walking with God" while the others
are not. And instead of the straightforward "and he died,"
which closes off the descriptions of other generations,
Enoch is said to have been "taken by God." The world
that the sages faced around 400 c.e., when Genesis
Rabbah was completed, was a world in which Christianity was ascending in power and popularity. This passage
might have been interpreted by Christians to indicate that
a righteous man who "walked with God" did not die but
could be taken directly to heaven as Elijah was supposed
to have done (2 Kings 2:1, 11) and as Jesus was supposed
to have ascended to heaven after his resurrection (Mark
16:19). To counter this argument, the sages point out that
when the text states that God "takes" a person, it means
simply "death" (as, for example, in Ezekiel 24:16). So
Rabbi Yose is eager to answer a question about this verse
with his own interpretation.

> A matron asked R. Yose [a question]. She said to him,
> "We do not find death [stated] of Enoch?" Said he to her:
> If it said, "and Enoch walked with God" (Genesis 5:24)
> and no more, I would agree with you. [Since, however,]
> it says, "and he was not for God took him," it means that
> he was no more in the world [having died], "for God took
> him." (*Genesis Rabbah, Bereishit* 25:1)

Here, Rabbi Yose applies the simple and often-used technique of supplying the end of a verse to answer a question.

This matron's question may reflect a point of contro-
versy between Christianity and Judaism and may have

been frequently asked in many contexts. Was this matron a Judeo-Christian, that is, a Jew who had become Christian and was therefore familiar with Jewish Scripture? Or was she a gentile Christian who was simply challenging a sage on his interpretation of a passage that, for her, explained one aspect of her faith? Or was she Jewish and seeking a way to answer Christian interpretations of this verse? It is impossible to say which identity this woman had and therefore we should not assume one answer to be correct. It seems equally plausible that this woman was a Christian challenging Judaism or that she was a Jew seeking a way to answer questions from Christians, or simply a Jew noticing an inconsistency in the text and seeking an explanation of it. Another possibility is that this matron is the collective personification of many women who studied Scripture and asked sages their questions. If this is the case, then this passage bespeaks a community of studying women whose existence is, by and large, ignored in our sources.

Another example of this phenomenon is the following interchange between a matron and R. Yose:

> A matron asked R. Yose b. Halafta [a question]. She said to him, "Why did Esau issue first?" He said to her, "Because the first drop was Jacob's." [And] he said to her, "If you place two diamonds in a tube, does not the one put in first come out last? So also the first drop was [that which formed] Jacob." (*Genesis Rabbah*, *Toldot* 63:8)

As always, the context of this passage is important to understanding its underlying significance. As Jacob Neusner has explained, *Genesis Rabbah* is a work that expresses a sustained point of view: the adaptation of the sages' Judaism to the realities of a Christian world.[1] The sages reinterpreted the Book of Genesis in a way that could explain to them, and other Jews, why Christianity appeared to have triumphed. To do this, the sages identified Jacob as Judaism and Esau as Christianity: fraternal twins in conflict. Given this framework, questions about the primacy of Esau over Jacob were interpreted as questions about the primacy of Christianity over Judaism. So a matron asking why Esau was born first is really asking why Christianity has triumphed over Judaism, as the firstborn child is expected to do. Rabbi Yose bar Halafta parries this question skillfully, suggesting that Jacob was the first conceived and so is the second born. Therefore, Judaism is really the true first son.

Again, we must ask ourselves, "Is the matron asking this question a Christian? Or is this matron a Jew seeking a way to answer the questions of Christians? Who is more likely to have known this text and asked a sage about it?" Once more, it seems equally plausible that the matron in this passage could be Jewish or Christian and so we should be careful in saying with surety, "This matron is definitely a non-Jew." The text simply does not support that conclusion unequivocally. Indeed, it would seem more logical that this woman is Jewish.

The matrons in these passages bear a strong resemblance to a type of Jewish matron today. There are many Jewish women (and they have numerous male counterparts) whose attachment to, and curiosity about, Judaism is strongest when they are challenged by the non-Jewish world around them about that Judaism. These are Jews who rarely attend services or study a Jewish text. However, when Christian groups begin proselytizing in their neighborhoods or the songs the chorus sings at the

winter concert are too religiously Christian, they will immediately appeal to their rabbi to help them combat what
they perceive to be an attack on their Judaism. In some
ways, it is sad that this is what is most alive for them in
their Judaism. However, at least *something* in their Judaism is alive and can serve as a basis on which to build a
more diversified approach to their Jewishness.

Yet another example of this phenomenon of a woman
who is well versed in Jewish Scripture asking R. Yose a
question is found in this passage:

> A matron asked [a question] of R. Yose. She said to him,
> "Is it possible that Joseph, at seventeen years of age, with
> all the hot blood of youth, could act thus?" He [there-
> upon] brought before her the Book of Genesis and began
> reading before her the story of Reuben and Bilhah and
> the story of Judah and Tamar. He said to her, "If [con-
> cerning] these, who were older and under their fathers'
> authority, Scripture did not conceal anything about them,
> how much the more in the case of Joseph, who was
> young and his own master." (*Genesis Rabbah*, *Vayeishev*
> 87:6)

This interchange revolves around the following incident
in the Torah:

> And it came to pass after these things that his master's
> wife cast her eyes upon Joseph and she said: "Lie with
> me." But he refused and said unto his master's wife:
> "Behold, my master, having me, knows not what is in the
> house, and he has put all that he has into my hand; he is
> not greater in this house than I; neither has he kept back
> anything from me but you, because you are his wife. How
> then can I do this great wickedness, and sin against God?"

> And it came to pass, as she spoke to Joseph day by day
> that he hearkened not unto her, to lie by her, or to be
> with her. (Genesis 39:7–10)

The matron cannot believe that a hot-blooded teenager
of seventeen could refuse the sexual advances of a woman
day after day. R. Yose's reply is that the Torah is forthright in describing how Reuven slept with Bilhah, his
father's concubine, while his father was still alive (Genesis 35:22), which was shameful behavior, and how Judah
refused to allow his son to marry his childless, widowed,
daughter-in-law as the laws of levirate marriage demand
(Genesis 38:1–30). If the Torah is forthright about these
shameful stories, it stands to reason that it would openly
describe Joseph's acquiescence to seduction if he had,
indeed, acquiesced. However, since the Torah is willing
to report when others did not resist sin, and it reports that
Joseph did resist, we can be confident that Joseph did,
in fact, resist the temptation to sleep with Potiphar's wife.
Once more we note that there is nothing in her question
that identifies this matron as Jewish or non-Jewish and
so both possibilities must be considered as plausible. Indeed, this question has no readily apparent connection
with Christianity or paganism at all.

We find yet another example of a matron asking a
question of R. Yose bar Halafta on a point of Scripture:

> One matron asked R. Yose bar Halafta [a question]. She
> said to him, "What means that which is said, 'He gives
> wisdom unto the wise (Daniel 2:21)'? The text should
> have stated, 'He gives wisdom unto them that are not wise
> and knowledge to them that know not understanding'!"
> He said to her, "[I will explain with] a parable. If two per-
> sons come to borrow money from you, one rich and the

other poor, to whom would you lend, the rich man or the poor?" She said to him, "To the rich man." He said to her, "Why?" She said to him, "Because if the rich man loses my money he has wherewith to repay me; but if the poor man loses my money, from where can he repay me?" He said to her, "Do your ears hear what you have uttered with your mouth? If the Holy One, blessed be He, gave wisdom to fools, they would sit and meditate upon it in privies, theaters, and bathhouses; but the Holy One, blessed be He, gave wisdom to the wise who sit and meditate upon it in Synagogues and Houses of Study. Hence, 'He gives wisdom unto the wise and knowledge to them that know understanding' (Daniel 2:21)" (*Ecclesiastes Rabbah* 1:7 ¶ 5)

The matron's question seems logical. The verse from Daniel does strike one as odd at first. R.Yose does an elegant job of explaining the verse. God gives wisdom, that is, Torah, only to the wise because God can rely on wise persons to follow proper etiquette when studying Torah. In general, the sages felt that one should not study words of Torah or repeat them in places of filth or secular entertainment. Once more we note that this matron could be Jewish or Christian or pagan. We also note that the text seems to imply that this woman was wealthy, and with sharp business sense, to boot. This also fits the picture we are developing of wealthy women who were deeply involved in their religious institutions.

Women's Study Groups Then and Now

What can we discern from these passages? Perhaps such matrons never existed and are simply literary devices constructed by the sages. This is the most frequently suggested explanation for their appearance in rabbinic literature. The sages might, perhaps, be "role playing" theological discussions between Jews and non-Jews to help Jews prepare for such situations. If this is the case, we then wonder why the non-Jew is personified as a woman rather than as a man, and we have no obvious answer for this question. Another possibility for the matron's appearance in these passages is that there was a group of women, Jewish, Judeo-Christian, gentile-Christian, or pagan, who studied Jewish Scripture intensely and came to Rabbi Yose bar Halafta to have their questions answered. Let us just imagine that this latter scenario actually occurred (naturally, we cannot discern the definitive answer to our questions). That would mean that the women's study groups we see today are not anomalous or revolutionary. They would have historical precedent behind them. And the fact that some rabbis reject such study by women while others encourage it has the precedent of Rabbi Eliezer on the one hand and Rabbi Yose bar Halafta on the other. These passages do seem to suggest that women were as interested in Torah study as men, just as they are today, and asked penetrating, perceptive questions about the text.

The Non-Jewish (?) Matron

We do have one story involving a matron and Rabbi Yose that identifies the matron as a non-Jew. However, we should exercise great caution before leaping to the conclusion that this means every time a matron is mentioned it refers to a non-Jewish woman, especially since the part

of the passage that identifies her as a non-Jew (in paren-
theses, below) is missing from some versions of the text.
This passage differs from all the others we have considered so far in that it is *not* based on a discussion of a
Jewish text but rather a straightforward theological question. If anything, this would seem to support the idea that
the matron asking about a Torah text could be Jewish
while a matron asking questions without referring to a
Jewish text is non-Jewish. If the term matron refers to a
social class of women, perhaps wealthy, widowed women,
then this class could equally well contain Jewish and non-
Jewish members as the class "society matron" does today.
We note once more that there is no reason that the protagonist of the tale need be a woman. A man could fill
the role equally well.

This passage may be seen as addressing the question
of dualism in Judaism. Stated in its simplest terms, the
dualistic system of religious belief associated the body
with death, decay, and impurity. The spirit was associated
with immortality, eternity, and purity. These two forces
battled against each other. The God of the Torah is un-
ambiguously identified as the God who made creation,
that is, the physical world. Dualists wondered how this God
who was associated with the physical world could be associated with the world of the spirit as well. This is the theological context for the following tale:

A matron asked [a question of] R. Yose bar Halafta. She
said to him, "In how many days did the Holy One, Blessed
be He, create the world?" He said to her, "In six days."
She said to him, "What has He been doing since then until
now?" He said to her, "The Holy One, Blessed be He, has
been making matches: the daughter of so-and-so to so-

and-so. The wife of so-and-so to so-and-so." She said to him, "This is the extent of His art?! I can do the same thing. How many menservants, how many maidservants do I have! In no time at all, I can match them up." He said to her, "If [this is] easy in your eyes, it is as hard for the Holy One, Blessed be He, as splitting the Red Sea."

R. Yose bar Halafta went away. What did she do? She took a thousand menservants and a thousand maidservants, lined them up in row upon row facing one another, and she said, "This man shall marry that woman, and this woman shall marry that man," and so she matched them all up in a single night. The next day, the ones thus matched came to the lady, one with his head bloodied, one with her eye knocked out, another with her leg broken. She said to them, "What [happened] to you?" One woman said, "I don't want that man," and a man said, "I don't want that woman."

(Immediately she sent to have R. Yose bar Halafta brought to her. She said to him, "My gods are not like your God. Your Torah is true, pleasant, worthy, and worthy of praise.") (*Genesis Rabbah* 68:4)

This evidently extremely wealthy matron is taught a lesson in human relations and theology by Rabbi Yose. In this object lesson, God appears not only as the God of physicality (producing the six days of creation) but also the God of the heart and spirit (who unites couples in love). She is impressed by the God Rabbi Yose espouses and also the Torah, which is the basis of Rabbi Yose's teachings. However, this phenomenon is not reported in every version of this story. We also note that she calls God "the Holy One, Blessed be He" at the very beginning of the tale, a distinctly Jewish way of naming God. We can think of it in the following modern terms. Would a Christian asking a Jew about God be more likely to refer to the Deity as God or as, for example, *Ribono shel Olam*, the Master of the Universe? We suspect the former is more likely to be the case than the latter.

The Matron in the Bavli

In our sources that come from Babylonia, as opposed to those we have already studied that came from the Land of Israel, the matron is not described as learning with the sages but as a figure of action and influence. For example, the matron in our next passage is effective in ensuring that a righteous gentile, Keti'ah bar Shalom, who tried to save Jews from a vicious Roman ruler, is able to enter the World to Come.

> [Keti'ah bar Shalom] was being held and led away [for execution]; a matron said of him: Pity the ship that sails [toward the harbor] without paying the tax. Then, throwing himself on his foreskin he cut it away and said: You have paid the tax; you will pass and enter [paradise]. (B. *Avodah Zarah* 10b)

Keti'ah bar Shalom argued against the persecution of the Jews and for this he was condemned to death. On the way to his execution, this matron alludes to the fact that he is uncircumcised and therefore may not be eligible to enter the World to Come. He thereupon circumcises himself and "pays the tax" to enter Paradise. Once more, we must ask ourselves what is more logical, that a non-Jewish woman would urge a non-Jewish man to circumcise himself in order to enter Paradise or that a Jewish woman would do so? It seems far more logical that a Jewish woman would urge a non-Jewish man, sympathetic to Jewish causes, to observe a *mitsvah* and so be able to enter (the Jewish conception of) the World to Come. Would a pagan woman be sympathetic to this man at all? Wouldn't a Christian woman be more likely to urge that he accept Jesus before death? The most logical alternative seems to point to the woman being a Jew. In addition, there seems to be no reason to think that a man could not, perhaps even more credibly, have urged Keti'ah bar Shalom to circumcise himself. Again, we find no compelling reason that these words must be said by a woman and thus it makes it relatively more likely that a woman did, in fact, say them.

In another example of the way matrons are portrayed in the *Bavli*, we find that one matron has the political savvy the sages need to help the Jewish community.

> The evil government [of Rome] had issued a decree that they should not study the Torah and that they should not circumcise their sons and that they should profane the Sabbath. What did Judah ben Shammu'a and his colleagues do? They went and consulted a certain matron around whom all the great ones of Rome gathered. She said to them: Go and make proclamation [of your sorrows] at night time. They went and proclaimed at night, crying, "In heaven's name, are we not your brothers, and are we not the sons of one father and are we not the sons of one mother? Why are we different from every nation and tongue that you issue such harsh decrees against us?" [The decrees were thereupon] annulled and that day was declared a feast day. (B. *Rosh Hashanah* 19a // B. *Taanit* 18a)

Clearly, this matron was able to give the sages effective advice. Who is more likely to have given the sages help, a Jewish woman or a pagan woman? It seems relatively more likely that a Jewish woman would help the Jewish community. This passage also fits the picture we are developing of a wealthy, influential woman. Perhaps she curried favor with the Roman rulers in an elegant "salon" atmosphere and thus knew what would work to influence them. Once more, we must note that the protagonist of the tale could easily have been an influential male civic leader.

This cannot be said of the following passage, which would not function with a man as the central character. This story is the third part of a beautiful tripartite passage about giving people the benefit of the doubt.

Our rabbis taught: One time students of the sages needed something from a matron around whom all the great men of Rome were to be found. Said they, "Who will go?" Rabbi Joshua said to them, "I will go." Rabbi Joshua and his students went. When he reached the door of her house, he removed his *tefillin* at a distance of four cubits, entered, and shut the door in front of them. After he came out he descended, had a ritual bath, and learned with his students. And he said to them, "When I removed my *tefillin*, of what did you suspect me?" "We said, 'Perhaps Rabbi reasons, "Let not sacred words enter a place of uncleanness."'" "When I shut [the door], of what did you suspect me?" "We said, 'Perhaps he has [to discuss] an affair of state with her.'" "When I descended and had a ritual bath, of what did you suspect me?" "We said, 'Perhaps some spittle spurted from her mouth upon the Rabbi's garments.'" He said to them, "[By the Temple] service it was just so. And you—just as you judged me favorably, so may the Omnipresent judge you favorably." (B. *Shabbat* 127b)

In the case of this tale we understand that we need a woman character. Otherwise, there would be no reason for anyone to think anything scandalous of Rabbi Joshua taking off his *tefillin* (as one would do before having intercourse), closing the door (ditto) and ritually immersing himself upon leaving before studying Torah (as he would have done after having sexual relations). His students, however, did not allow themselves to be scandalized and judged every suspicious act in the most favorable light. The matron in this story serves as little more than a literary device to introduce possible scandal into the story so that the value of giving someone the benefit of the doubt may be illustrated. Was this matron Jewish or Roman? We simply are not given enough information in this story to determine the answer and it would seem reckless to offer an opinion with certainty when such certainty cannot be achieved from the sources.

All these passages point to the matron as a member of a social class: wealthy, independent, influential, knowledgeable, quite-possibly *Jewish* women. Such women would have been a natural counterpart to their pagan and Christian equals. In the *Bavli*, they are not portrayed as studying Torah. This could be because they did not study in Babylonia. Or the Babylonian sages could have repressed or ignored materials about women studying Torah. The *Bavli* is willing to portray matrons as socially powerful but not as engaging in study; our sources from the Land of Israel portray them as studying and de-emphasize their power. Were the roles of matrons different in these different locales or do these phenomena reflect the biases of the sages in these two places? It is impossible, now, to know.

Why Did Scholars "Erase" the Matron?

In almost all these "matron" passages, we again note that there is no reason that the person asking the question needed to be a woman. Each of the questions, whether related to Jewish texts or not, could have been as logically asked by a man as by a woman. There is no obvious connection to women's issues in these questions; they seem to be general textual and theological questions. It therefore makes it seem more likely that such a class of women, interested in studying religious issues and probably wealthy, did exist, since it seems unlikely that the sages would fabricate tales about women when they could plausibly do so about men.

This leads us to another question. Why has it been almost universally assumed that the matron is a "straw woman," a literary invention of rabbinic literature? This assumption simply erases from existence what we have at least some reason to believe is a group of women devoted to Torah study with the sages. Was it easier for scholars of more recent generations to assume this was a fiction than to believe that women did study in the rabbinic era? Why did they not consider the at least plausible possibility that there was a group of Jewish women studying with Rabbi Yose ben Halafta? Was this something modern scholars simply couldn't believe? It is difficult to know the answer to our questions. As always, we must remember that our sources speak on many levels and we can most fully appreciate them when we are open to all their possible interpretations, whether those interpretations are consistent with our preconceived notions or not.

The existence of these women, and their apparent interest in Torah study, should not be dismissed as a literary invention of the sages. Such an explanation of their appearance in our sources is a way of silencing their voices. If the sages of rabbinic literature did not want to deny their existence, then why should we?

3

Entering and Exiting Relationships: Theory versus Practice

Dealing with Anger at the Sources

In the introduction, we briefly mentioned the fact that many women, and men, encountering rabbinic texts for the first time, and for a good while thereafter, are angered by the sexism they see in these texts. There are many possible responses to this anger. We could simply reject rabbinic literature in toto, saying, "If it contains this sort of sexism, none of it can be good." This is like a person who eats a peach pit and throws away the fruit. We may thereby reduce our encounters with rabbinic sexism, but we'll have lost all the wonderful things that this literature can teach us, as well. One way of dealing with these attitudes in the texts is to develop an understanding of the different sorts of rabbinic literature so that we can comprehend each passage appropriately.

Of course, no one is denying that there are sexist statements in rabbinic literature. However, when we understand that statements in the *Mishnah* tend to be global and theoretical and comments in the *Gemara* tend to be more down to earth we can begin to see in rabbinic literature a more holistic, realistic, and egalitarian attitude toward women than when we read the sages' comments without considering their context. In this chapter, we have many opportunities to contrast the *Mishnah*'s theoretical teachings about women with the way women are reported to have behaved in the *Gemara*. When we consider these two sources separately, we find that women and men rarely, it seems, behaved according to the idealistic dictates of the *Mishnah* when getting married or divorced. The contrast between the *Mishnah*'s view of these transitional moments and that of the other works of rabbinic literature is sort of like the difference between the public performance of a wedding ceremony and a "behind the scenes" look at all the preparations, aggravations, mistakes, and tribulations that go into making the public ceremony so orderly. In the synagogue, everyone is in place, everyone knows what to do and does it in an orderly fashion. Behind the scenes, there are worries about flowers, dresses, food, and what to wrap the glass in so that when it is stepped on the shards won't fly everywhere.

The *Mishnah*'s Ideal

This contrast between the *Mishnah* and the *Gemara* is not surprising. Transitions are, by their very nature, messy, complicated things, especially when they concern love and disaffection as do betrothal and divorce. That is why rituals come to be attached to these moments—so that their unpredictability can be regulated. We have a basic contrast, in rabbinic literature and in life, between the "storybook" versions of weddings and divorces and the way weddings and divorces actually happen. For example, in the *Mishnah*, transitions from a single state to marriage and back again are portrayed as simple, orderly ones:

> The woman is acquired in three ways and she acquires herself in two ways. She is acquired by money, by a document, or by sexual relations. By money: the House of Shammai says by one *dinar* or by one *dinar's* worth. The House of Hillel says by a *perutah* or by one *perutah's* worth. And how much is a *perutah* [worth]? One eighth of an Italian *issar*. And she acquires herself by a divorce document or by the death of her husband. The *yevamah* (widowed sister-in-law) is acquired by sexual relations and acquires herself by [the ceremony of] *chalitsah* and the death of the brother-in-law. (M. *Kiddushin* 1:1)

It all sounds so simple. A woman is married in three ways (the term acquired here doesn't mean she is "bought" but rather that a man acquires the right to have sexual intercourse with her in exchange for financially supporting her): (1) through the exchange of money (the man gives the woman a more valuable coin [Beit Shammai's opinion] or a less-valuable coin [Beit Hillel's opinion]), (2) by a written agreement (the wedding document, the *ketubah*), and (3) through sexual relations (a man sleeps with a woman with the intent to be married and that means they are married). To get out of a marriage, a woman can receive a divorce or her husband can die. A *yevamah*, that is, a woman whose husband died and left her childless, is obligated to marry her husband's brother and produce an heir in the dead brother's stead. If she does not wish to marry her brother-in-law or he refuses to marry her, she can be released from this obligation through the ceremony of chalitsah (a sort of anticommitment ceremony) and/or through the death of her brother-in-law. These rules seem simple, clear, and direct. They also appear to allocate to the woman an extremely passive role. She is "acquired" and must wait on a man's decision or his death to be married or released from marriage.

Ancient Sexual Harassment

How different do these transitional moments appear when they involve accounts of what women actually *did* during these processes! Women took very active roles in their engagements, weddings, divorces, and entanglements with the laws of chalitsah. For example, apparently it was not uncommon for men to attempt to betroth women when the women really weren't interested in becoming betrothed. And women were free to reject such proposals. In the following passage we find three examples of women rejecting such propositions:

> A man was selling (9a) glass beads when a woman came and said to him, "Give me a string [of these]." He said to her, "If I give it to you will you become betrothed to me?" She said to him, "Oh, indeed, do give it to me." Said Rav Hama: Every [such expression,] "Oh, indeed, do give it to me" means nothing.
>
> A man was drinking wine in a tavern when a woman came and said to him, "Give me a cup." He said to her, "If I give it to you will you become betrothed to me?" She said to him, "Oh, indeed, do give me a drink." Said Rav

Hama: Every [such expression,] "Oh, indeed, do give it to me" means nothing.

A man was throwing down dates from a palm tree when a woman came and said to him, "Throw me down two." He said to her, "If I throw them down to you will you become betrothed to me?" She said to him, "Oh, indeed, throw them down." Said Rav Z'vid: Every [such expression], "Oh, indeed, throw them down" means nothing. (B. *Kiddushin* 8b–9a)

These three stories are only a very small part of the commentary on our *mishnah*'s (M. *Kiddushin* 1:1) statement that a woman can be acquired by anything of value. The sages set up elaborate rules to govern the transition of a woman into a married state through the transfer of money. It was not enough for a man to simply throw something worth a few coins at a woman and say, "How about it? Want to get married?" The transaction had to be effected with a maximum of seriousness and dignity. He had to give her the money, or its equivalent (today it is usually a ring), and declare, "Behold, you are consecrated unto me" and she had to consent, that is, accept the money.

Part of the betrothal process was the wedding document, the *ketubah*. In ancient days, long before the rabbinic era, a husband would pay a price for a bride. Eventually, instead of having to pay this money "up front," the bride price was written into the wedding contract as a lien against the man's property in case of divorce. This had two beneficial effects: (1) it meant that even poor men could marry and (2) it meant a man had to have money to divorce and that this money would go to the wife as financial support after the divorce. The *ketubah* benefited the woman in two ways. First, it prevented precipitous divorces because the man knew how much the settlement would cost and it was usually quite a bit of money in the sages' days. Second, the divorce settlement was drawn up when the man wanted the woman the most, not when he wanted her the least.

What happened in the three cases in our passage? In each case, a woman makes a simple request of a man and he uses this request as an opportunity to try to become engaged to the woman. And in each case, the woman simply dismisses the man's actions as nonsense or an irritation. Interestingly, it seems that these cases were brought before sages to rule on whether the women had become betrothed and in each case the sages side with the women: men are not allowed to harass women with unwanted proposals when all the women want to do is conduct legitimate business. These scenarios are a far cry from the orderly world the *Mishnah* described. In the *Mishnah*, the woman is passive. Here, the women are able to stick up for themselves and their rights in fending off unwanted advances.

Today, we might see an ancient form of sexual harassment in these stories. The women are just trying to do business and the men insist on making sexual suggestions in the process. The sages denounce such behavior emphatically. A woman need not put up with, or be bound by, such crass behavior. It is interesting, too, that these stories depict the relationship between the sexes more accurately than the modern media. While it is men who are generally more desperate to wed (and who benefit most from marriage) the media portray women as the ones who are desperately searching for spouses. (Several years ago women over forty were told that they were more likely to be the victims of a terrorist attack than be brides.)

These stories from the *Gemara* show how eager these men were to marry and how uninterested the women were. The *Gemara* seems to show that this dynamic has not changed over the centuries . . . and reports on it more accurately than our own contemporary media!

Becoming Engaged

While the *Mishnah*'s idealistic system may have occasionally worked out in real life, our next passage shows how complicated a process betrothal actually was. The *Mishnah* states that a girl who is no longer a little girl but is not yet considered a woman (a *naarah*, between twelve and twelve and a half years old) can be betrothed by her father or her father's representative (M. *Kiddushin* 2:1). This is as opposed to a woman (older than twelve and a half years old) who can become betrothed through herself or through an agent, just as a man can. The sages of the *Mishnah*, in attempting to deal with the troublesome, liminal time of puberty, appear to opt for entrusting a blossoming girl's status to her father's care. This sounds logical and sensible. However, as we might guess, when dealing with a young woman's romantic entanglements, little is clear cut or easily dealt with and, indeed, the following cases from the *Gemara* to this mishnah bear this out:

> A certain man betrothed [a minor] with a bunch of vegetables in a marketplace. Said Ravina, Even for the one who says that we fear lest her father consented, that is only [when it is done] in an honorable manner, but not in a contemptuous manner. Rav Aha of Difti said to Ravina: What is a contempt[uous way]? The vegetables

or [the fact that it was done in] a marketplace? The practical difference arises if he betroths her with money in the
marketplace or with a bunch of vegetables at home. What
then? He said, "Both the [former] and [the latter] are
contemptuous."

A certain man said, "[Our minor daughter must be
married] to my relation"; whereas she [his wife] said, "To
my relation." She nagged him until he said to her that she
could be [married] to her relation. While they were eating and drinking [to celebrate the girl's betrothal to the
mother's relation, that is, before the betrothal actually took
place], his relation went up to a loft and betrothed her
[and this case came before the sages]. Said Abaye: It is
written, "The remnant of Israel shall not do iniquity nor
speak lies" (Zephaniah 3:13). Rava said: It is a presump-
tion that he does not trouble to prepare a banquet and
then destroy it. Wherein do they differ? They differ in the
case where he did not trouble. (B. *Kiddushin* 45b)

The sages of the Babylonian Talmud were not composing a philosophical, idealistic document as were the sages
of the *Mishnah*. They revealed the messiness of reality
when contrasted with the elegance of law. In the first case,
a girl who is still under her father's control is walking
through the marketplace and suffers the (unwanted) ad-
vance of a man who attempts to betroth her in a very
uncouth manner. (Imagine today that someone tried to
betroth a woman at a baseball game by offering to buy
her a pretzel and a glass of beer.) This man's act is disqualified on any number of grounds by the sages. First
of all, even if this girl's father agreed to this betrothal, he
certainly didn't agree for it to take place in this undignified manner. This betrothal is considered invalid for two
reasons: (1) because of the inappropriate venue and (2)

because of the inappropriate material. Even if the vegetables were worth a *perutah*, this was not considered a legitimate means of betrothal, just as a cigar band is hardly considered a valid wedding band today even though it is a band with which one might technically be wed. Then the broader question of Jewish law is addressed: what if he had given her a real ring in the marketplace or vegetables at home; in other words, he had tried the betrothal with the right material in the wrong place or the wrong material in the right place? Ravina rules that everything has to be right: the father has to have consented and it must be the right material and the right place. In other words, not only does the father still control the girl's status, in line with the *Mishnah*'s ruling, but everything must be done with proper decorum as well. The girl in this passage does not seem to play an active role, or perhaps her role simply was not documented. (She might have wanted to marry this man and this "undignified" form of betrothal could have been her way of eloping.)

The second part of our passage shows that while the *Mishnah* may have assigned all rights to betroth a daughter to a father, mothers had a great deal to say about the process. How reassuring to know that these moments of transition seem to have involved family conflict then as well as now! Once the father capitulated to the mother's wishes, they made a banquet that preceded the actual betrothal. However, while everyone was rejoicing, the father's relative sneaked upstairs and betrothed the girl to himself. Abaye relies on the father's personal integrity as a pretext whereby he may reject the clandestine betrothal. That is, Abaye assumes that the father has not given consent to his (the father's) relative to betroth his daughter because Abaye assumes that Jews do not lie so despicably and uses the verse from Zephaniah as proof that Jews do not lie so. Rava, on the other hand, bases his ruling that the betrothal is not valid on monetary considerations: the father would not have spent so much money on this betrothal party just to have it spoiled by this unwelcome surprise. What is the practical difference between these two rulings of Abaye and Rava? What if the father did not give an expensive party? In that case, Rava fears that the father might well have consented to the clandestine betrothal.

We can think of this case in the following modern terms. Which bride's father would be more likely to be angry if his daughter eloped? The father of a bride who had spent $100,000 on a wedding or one who had spent $100? We suspect the former father might be somewhat more put out if his daughter eloped because of all the funds he had expended for the wedding. The father who had only spent $100 might be less upset since he had spent less money in planning the wedding.

In both cases, the *Mishnah*'s dignified system scarcely describes the confusing behavior of young people in love. They act impulsively or in an undignified manner. Those who supposedly have no power (e.g., the mother of a girl) actually wield quite a bit of influence. The *Mishnah*'s elegant system barely correlates with the way people actually behaved.

Irregular Betrothals

One more example of the way in which the *Mishnah*'s rulings about betrothals fit (or don't fit) with real life may be brought. Here we have a rare case where a real-life situation is mentioned within the *Mishnah* itself.

> If one betroths a woman and her daughter or a woman and her sister simultaneously, they are not betrothed. And it once happened to five women, among whom were two sisters, that a man gathered a basket of figs, which was theirs, and which was of the seventh year [and therefore ownerless], and he said, "Behold, you are all betrothed unto me with this basket." And one accepted it on behalf of all of them. The sages said, the sisters are not betrothed. (M. *Kiddushin* 2:7)

This ruling in the *Mishnah* is based on the following verses from the Torah:

> You shall not uncover the nakedness of a woman and her daughter; you shall not take her son's daughter, or her daughter's daughter, to uncover her nakedness; they are near kinswomen; it is lewdness. And you shall not take a woman to her sister, to be a rival to her, to uncover her nakedness, beside the other in her lifetime. (Leviticus 18:17–18)

These rules seem to be based on basic human decency and the *Mishnah* simply repeats these prohibitions from the Torah. The example in the *Mishnah* seems a little puzzling. How could one man propose marriage to five women at the same time? And why did they all accept? Was he exceptionally good looking or well off? Were men and women in the habit of behaving this way or was this a special man or a special moment in history? Perhaps this tale was so odd that it was remembered as more conventional betrothals were not. At any rate, the two sisters were not betrothed by this man's act, in accord with the *Mishnah*'s ruling that two sisters cannot be betrothed to one man at the same time, so only three of the women became betrothed to this man.

There is another problem with this betrothal that makes it unconventional. A woman cannot be betrothed with something that belongs to her, as today one does not become engaged by wearing one's own cocktail ring as an engagement ring. Did some of the figs in the basket belong to the women and therefore could not be used for betrothal? The figs were produce of the Sabbatical year and therefore considered ownerless. This needs some explanation. Every seven years the land was to be given rest and not farmed and this was called the Sabbatical year (Exodus 23:10–11, Leviticus 25:2–7, Deuteronomy 15:1–3). Produce of such a year was considered ownerless and so could be claimed and used validly as the monetary equivalent for a betrothal, which is what the man in our story did.

This mishnah touches on a point rarely discussed in rabbinic literature: the relationship of sisters to each other. The sages explore relationships between men and women and among men but the relationships among women are a sort of "blind spot" for them. Those women who have sisters are aware of the great solidarity, as well as the ferocious competition, such relationships can engender. We cannot know how these sisters felt about each other, but it is entertaining to speculate on the characters in this case.

The *Gemara* to this mishnah in the *Bavli* explores further what happens when a man attempts to betroth a woman with material or money that is not clearly his own.

A certain woman was washing her feet in a bowl of water. A man came, snatched a *zuz* from his neighbor, threw it to her and said to her, "You are betrothed unto me!" Then that man went before Rava [for judgment]. He said, "None pay regard to Rabbi Shimon's dictum, viz.: Robbery in general involves the owner's abandonment."

A certain tenant farmer (who paid a percentage of his crops in rent) betrothed [a woman] with a handful of onions. He came before Rava [for judgment]. He said to him, "Who renounced [these onions] to you? (If the owner of the field did not grant them to the tenant then they are stolen property.)" Now, that applies only to a handful; but as for a bunch, he [the tenant farmer] can say to him [the landowner], "As I have taken a bunch, do you take one: one bunch is the same as another."

A certain spirits brewer betrothed [a woman] with a measure of beer. Then the owner of the beer came and found him. Said he to him, "Why did you not give [her] of this [beer, which is] stronger?" When he came before Rava, he said . . . she is not betrothed. (B. *Kiddushin* 52b)

These three stories are similar to the story in the *Mishnah*. All three involve women who are betrothed with material whose ownership is questionable. In the first case, the man apparently steals a silver coin and tries to use it to betroth a woman who is in an awkward position in the first place. A betrothal cannot take place with stolen property; this is obvious. So what is the question? The question is, "When do people give up hope of getting their stolen property back?" Rabbi Shimon holds that once people are robbed they give up hope of retrieving their property, that is, they abandon hope. If the owner has abandoned hope then the property would belong to the thief and actions taken with that money would be valid.

However, Rava rules that no attention is paid to Rabbi Shimon's principle in this case and that the betrothal is invalid.

In the second case, the tenant farmer betroths the woman with a bunch of onions. The owner of the field has not formally granted him ownership of exactly these onions, so there is some question as to whether the betrothal is valid. However, since the onions of one field are likely to be quite similar, and since these onions are destined to be divided between the tenant farmer and the landowner, there is no difficulty with this betrothal and it is considered valid. In other words, if the tenant farmer is allowed to keep one fourth of the produce from the field, it is not certain that these exact onions were from that one fourth. However, we know that the farmer would receive *some* onions, so we may presume that these are part of them.

The last case is similar to that of the tenant farmer. The brewer does not own the brewery or the beer, but he betroths the woman with the beer anyway. When the owner of the brewery discovers what has happened, he asks why the agent brewer did not betroth the woman with stronger (i.e., finer) spirits. The question before Rava is, "Is the betrothal valid even though the agent brewer did not own the beer?" Rava rules that it is not valid, taking the owner's question as a subtle objection to the agent's having taken the beer without permission. This can be likened to a man who works in a brewery and steals a six-pack of beer in order to betroth a woman. He is not entitled to the six-pack and his boss, when he discovers the transgression, instead of chiding the worker directly, says, "Gee, you might have bought her a ring, instead," implicitly indicating that he shouldn't have taken the six-pack for this purpose.

We might wonder who brought these cases to Rava. Was it the women themselves? If so, they probably wanted Rava to rule that the betrothals were invalid; otherwise they would simply have accepted the proposals. Or did the owners of the "stolen" property with which the women were betrothed bring these cases to Rava? In any case, we see once more how the *Gemara* preserves material about actual human behavior that does not exactly fit the *Mishnah*'s elegant philosophical system of prescriptions.

Irregular Betrothals Today

We should note that human nature has not changed much in the last fifteen hundred years. Rarely does the "storybook" proposal take place. Supposedly, the man comes, on bended knee, with a ring, and asks a woman to marry him. However, today betrothal tends to be a more protracted process. Couples often live together for a while before formally deciding to wed. Men rarely ask the father's permission to wed the daughter. Women frequently broach the topic of marriage first. Indeed, some couples seem to be married to each other on an emotional level almost immediately after they meet, while other couples don't seem wedded, even after years of marriage. Given these modern realities, with which we are all familiar, it is amazing that the "storybook" version still survives as an ideal. This distinction between "ideal" and real life is quite similar to the difference between the *Mishnah* and the *Gemara*, and we must take care to read our sources with this distinction in mind.

Martha's Marriage

Yet another special sort of betrothal is dealt with in the *Mishnah*: the betrothal of a high priest. The *kohanim*, the priests, were an aristocratic class who officiated at the Temple cult. Those priests who were appointed high priests were subject to some restrictions in terms of the women they could marry. Basically, they could marry only virgins, thus disqualifying widows from marrying high priests. However, the *Mishnah* preserves the tale of one widow who became betrothed to a priest who then became high priest and the marriage was considered valid.

> A high priest must not marry a widow. . . . If he betrothed a widow and was [then] appointed high priest he consummates the marriage. It once happened with Joshua ben Gamla that he betrothed Martha the daughter of Boethus and the king appointed him high priest, and he consummated the marriage. . . . (M. *Yevamot* 6:4)

First of all, who was Joshua ben Gamla? We have some evidence of Joshua's historical existence since he is mentioned by Josephus, a Jewish historian (*Antiquities* 20: 213). Joshua, like the sages, emphasized education as crucial (B. *Bava Batra* 21a) and was opposed to the zealots who battled the Romans in the siege of Jerusalem. He died in 69 or 70 c.e.

Second, who was Martha? Martha (d. 70 c.e.), the daughter of Boethus, is, in rabbinic literature, the archetype of an extremely rich woman, as the following passage from *Sifre*, an early commentary on the Book of Deuteronomy, attests:

> "Nor take the widow's raiment to pledge" (Deuteronomy 24:17): Whether she is poor or whether she is rich, even if she is [as rich] as Martha, daughter of Boethus. Rabbi Simeon says: When you take a pledge from a man, you may not return it to a woman, lest you should go back and forth to her home and thus tarnish her reputation. (*Sifre D. Piska* 281)

This is a comment on Deuteronomy 24:17: "You shall not pervert the justice due to the stranger, or to the fatherless, nor take the widow's raiment to pledge." This is a simple injunction not to oppress those who are unfortunate, a widow being a typical member of this category. In its interpretation of this verse, Sifre expands this injunction: we may not take a widow's raiment in pledge, even if she is rich. So the injunction becomes a general principle, not one based solely on compassion. What is interesting for our purposes is that Martha is so well known that she can be referred to as the example, par excellence, of a wealthy widow. Those who composed this passage were able to assume that every listener would understand what this reference to Martha meant, just as today we would instantly comprehend a mention of the name Jacqueline Onassis to refer to a very wealthy widow.

Martha seems to have been a member of the Boethusians. This was a group that probably originated with Simeon b. Boethus, who was appointed high priest by Herod the Great in 24 B.C.E. The Boethusians closely resembled the Sadducees and may have been a branch of them. The sages regarded the Boethusians as cynical priests who obtained their positions through bribes and who did not take the restrictions of their offices seriously.

So this Martha, a widow, was betrothed to a priest who then became high priest and was permitted to consummate the marriage. The *Gemara* fills in "the rest of the story," so to speak, of Martha's marriage to Joshua. Apparently, Joshua ben Gamla obtained some help from his new wife in becoming high priest.

> Said Rav Joseph, I see here a conspiracy; for Rav Assi, in fact, related that Martha the daughter of Boethus brought to King Yannai a basket of coins before he gave an appointment to Joshua ben Gamla among the high priests. (B. *Yevamot* 61a // B. *Yoma* 18a)

The king called Yannai here refers to Agrippa II (28–92 C.E.), the last king of the Herodian line. Apparently, Rav Assi suspected that Martha actually bribed the king to appoint Joshua high priest. We should note for the record that it was not uncommon in those days for high priests to be appointed because of their wealth. Therefore, there is nothing exactly inappropriate in Martha's marriage or her actions. She was betrothed to Joshua before he became a high priest and therefore they had the right to consummate the marriage, in line with the *Mishnah*. What Rav Assi seems to object to is the possibility that she bribed the king to make Joshua high priest, although Joshua seems to have been an individual who well deserved the honor.

Martha seems in these passages to be a wealthy, savvy woman, a woman who marries whom she wants and spends her money as she wants. She engineers her life and her relationships to suit her needs. (This stands in marked contrast to the legendary account of her death, which we will study in the chapter on loss.)

The sages seem to take a somewhat negative view of Martha, but we should be quite careful before jumping to the conclusion that it is because she is a woman or wealthy (or both). The sages have quite flattering things to say about other wealthy women, so their criticism may be based on her loyalties within the Jewish community. She is clearly allied with the priesthood, and the tension between the sages and the priestly class has been well documented. It could be this factor, rather than her gender, that causes the sages to view Martha negatively. We note, once more, that the *Mishnah* mandated one sort of behavior, but the human story that was shaped by that mandate was far more complicated and rich than the *Mishnah*'s somewhat dry prescriptions.

An Ancient Prenuptial Agreement

One of the thorniest issues related to marriage was the transition of a woman and her property from an independent state to one wherein her property was combined with her husband's property. In a quite detailed mishnah (M. *Ketubot* 8:1) the sages demonstrate how confusing these issues were for them and how poorly they fit into the neat paradigms outlined in the *Mishnah*. In general, the *Mishnah* rules that a woman may do what she wishes with that property she acquired before she became betrothed. In the *Gemara* to this mishnah, we learn of a case in which a woman used this ruling to her advantage.

A certain woman [a widow or divorcée who was about
to marry] wishing to deprive her [intended] husband of
her estate assigned it in writing to her daughter. She
married and was divorced. She came before Rav Nachman [to claim the return of her estate]. Rav Nachman
tore up the deed. Rav Anan, thereupon, went to Mar 'Ukba
and said to him, "See, Master, how Nachman the boor
tears up people's deeds." Mar 'Ukba said to him, "Tell
me, please, how exactly the incident occurred." He said
to him, "In such and such a manner." He said to him,
"Do you speak of a deed intended as a means of evasion?" Thus said Rav Hanilai bar Idi [in the name of]
Samuel: "I am an officially recognized judge, and should
a deed [which a woman] intended as a means of evasion come into my hand I would tear it up." (B. Ketubot
78b–79a)

Can a woman prevent her new husband from seizing
control of her property? The officially recognized answer
is, "Yes. She can do so." Even if she does so in a way that
is clearly meant to deprive her prospective husband of
any benefit from her property, she is allowed to make such
a transfer of property. The problem in this case is the
woman's daughter. Even though it was clear that when
the mother deeded her property to her daughter this was
simply a means of avoiding giving her new husband control over her property, the daughter is now contending that
the gift is valid and that the mother not be allowed to re-
trieve the property. Rav Nachman sides with the mother
in this case and tears up the deed: it was only meant as a
means of evasion and did not constitute an actual gift.

This is a situation that is associated with men more
often than women today. This is, in effect, an early form
of prenuptial agreement. We note that it is the *woman*,

not the man, who is making the prenuptial agreement and protecting her property. We have to wonder, though, about this woman. Why would she marry a man she didn't trust with her property? Perhaps it is comforting to know that fifteen hundred years ago, as today, people had doubts as they walked down the aisle, so to speak. And what kind of daughter did she raise who would so greedily cling to money that her mother had not truly intended her to have? We may have here a very early example of a "dysfunc-tional family." Indeed, money, then as now, can foul up family relationships to a remarkable extent. In this case, the woman's actions follow the *Mishnah*'s dictates while the daughter's would not have been predicted by the *Mish-nah*'s paradigms. Is this another example of the sages' "blind spot" regarding relationships between women? Or is this scenario so unusual that no one could have pre-dicted it or its outcome?

Divorce

Women took an active role not only in becoming be-trothed and married but in the processes of divorce and *chalitsah* as well. However, as was the case regarding marriage, the *Mishnah* portrays the woman's role as a passive one. For example, M. Gittin 4:1 focuses on a man's role in canceling a *get* (a Jewish divorce document) and does not mention a woman's role in the process at all.

> One who sends a *get* to his wife and he overtakes the messenger or sent another messenger after him [the first messenger] and said to him, "The *get* that I gave you is canceled," behold it is canceled. If he [the husband]

reached his wife before the messenger reached her and he said to her, "The *get* that I sent to you is canceled," behold it is canceled. If the *get* came into her hand, he is no longer able to cancel it. (M. *Gittin* 4:1)

From this mishnah we would never guess that the following incident could take place.

Giddal bar Re'ilai sent a *get* [a divorce decree] to his wife. The bearer went and found her weaving. He said to her, Here is your *get*. She said to him: Go away now at any rate and come again tomorrow. He [the messenger] went back to him [Giddal] and told him, whereupon he said, Blessed is He who is good and does good! (B. *Gittin* 34a)

This passage naturally makes us wonder about the relationship between Giddal bar Re'ilai and his wife. We know a good bit about Giddal. He was a Babylonian sage at the end of the third century and a student of Rav. He is portrayed as somewhat intense in his studies (B. *Shabbat* 30b); thus, it does not seem unlikely that he could send his wife a *get* in a fit of pique and be relieved when she rejects it, perhaps guessing that he is having a tantrum. That a sage's wife should simply dismiss her husband's divorce as irrelevant is not something we might expect when contemplating the *Mishnah*'s laws of divorce, which give virtually all of the power in this situation to the man. Indeed, we can easily imagine Giddal's wife: patient, mature, strong willed, and perhaps resigned to her flamboyant husband's antics.

Even today, while a woman has little formal role in the process of Jewish divorce, in actuality she can exercise a great deal of power in obtaining a *get*. While the woman stands passively and receives the divorce document during the actual ceremony, she may have been the one who instigated the divorce or even forced her husband into it. The human dynamics are not necessarily completely expressed through the ritual or described by the *Mishnah*.

Chalitsah

A woman could also take an active role in the process of *chalitsah*, disengaging herself from the obligation to marry the brother of her late husband. Until a woman could perform this rite, she was not free to marry anyone else. The practice of levirate marriage and *chalitsah* is outlined in the Torah.

> If brothers live together and one of them dies and he has no child, the wife of the dead man shall not be married abroad unto one who is not his kin. The brother of her dead husband shall go in unto her and take her to him to wife and perform the obligation of a husband's brother to her. And it shall be that the firstborn that she bears shall succeed in the name of his brother that is dead, so that his name not be blotted out in Israel. And if the man wish not to take his brother's wife, then his brother's wife shall go up to the gate unto the elders, and say, My husband's brother refuses to raise up unto his brother a name in Israel; he is unwilling to perform the obligation of a husband's brother unto me. Then shall the elders of the city call him, and speak unto him, and if he stand and say, I desire not to take her, then his brother's wife shall draw nigh unto him in the presence of the elders, and loose his shoe from off his foot and spit before his face; and she shall answer and say, So shall be done to

the man who will not build up his brother's house. (Deuteronomy 25:5–9)

This is obviously meant to be a degrading ritual for the man to go through. The *Mishnah* here (M. *Yevamot* 12:3–5) explores many theoretical possibilities that might invalidate or impair the correct performance of this ritual. These factors include the mental competence of the participating partners, whether the recitation of the prescribed formula (Deuteronomy 25:9) is accomplished correctly, and so forth. In the *Mishnah* these are explored as theoretical possibilities, but an actual case of a disabled woman's performance of *chalitsah* is brought in the *Gemara*.

> A man [and a woman who was his widowed sister-in-law] once came before Rabbi Chiyya bar Abba. He [Rabbi Chiyya bar Abba] said to her, "Stand up, my daughter." She said to him, "Say, 'Her sitting is her standing.'" He said to her, "Do you know this man?" She said to him, "Yes. It is her money that he saw and would like to spend it." He said to her, "Do you not like him then?" She said to him, "No." [The rabbi] said to [the *levir*], "Submit to her *chalitsah* and you will thereby wed her." After the latter had submitted to *chalitsah* at her hands he said to him, "Now she is ineligible to marry you; submit again to a proper *chalitsah* that she may be permitted to marry a stranger." (B. *Yevamot* 106a)

Here we have a case of a woman who finds her brother-in-law unacceptable as a husband. She feels that he wants to marry her only for her money. It will help us understand this passage to know that *chalitsah* given under a false assumption is still valid. (This is somewhat like the difference between what a car salesman tells you is in the contract of purchase and what the fine print in it actually says. Once you have signed the contract you are bound by it, even if you signed it thinking it said something else.) Rabbi Chiyya bar Abba senses that this man may be somewhat difficult and so makes him submit to the woman's *chalitsah*, telling him that this is a prerequisite to their being married. This is a classic "false assumption" under which to do *chalitsah*. Once she has accomplished this *chalitsah*, she and her brother-in-law are forbidden to marry each other. Rabbi Chiyya then makes him undergo a proper *chalitsah* so that she may be well and truly free of this man and able to marry another. In other words, Rabbi Chiyya basically deceives this man in order to free this woman. Even though the woman formally has little power in this situation, we see that, with the cooperation of a clever sage, her wishes are important and potent.

This case shows that a woman is able to have her preferences enforced by a sage using his technical knowledge of the law instead of having to submit passively to the will of men, as we so often assume women did. There is some question about the statement, "Her sitting is her standing." Either she is disabled or it is a metaphorical statement, that is, her "sitting" (rejecting marriage) is her "standing" (salvation).

This passage brings to mind the plight of the *agunah* today. An *agunah* is a woman whose husband has deserted her or has disappeared and may no longer be alive. Such a woman is not allowed to remarry unless witnesses to the man's death can be found. The sad situation of these women is a blight on the entire Jewish community. Would that the sages of today were as clever in finding solutions to these problems as Rabbi Chiyya bar Abba was in ameliorating this woman's situation!

In almost all of our cases of women entering and exiting relationships, we find a broader picture painted of women's roles in the *Gemara* than in the *Mishnah*. In the *Mishnah* women's roles may be ignored, while they are brought more fully to light in the *Gemara*. In addition, the *Mishnah* almost always frames issues in terms of theory and the *Gemara* explores how the real world interacts with the *Mishnah*'s theories. When we read about women in the *Mishnah* (or really, about any topic), we must remember the context of the material and, if possible, contrast it with the commentary of the *Gemara* in order to see a clearer picture of our subject. The picture of women that we find in the *Gemara* is of a complex group of people— some active, some passive—who are vitally involved in their relationships. In other words, these women are very much like Jewish women today.

4

Virtue as Power I: Husband–Wife Relationships

The Power of Virtue

When a group of people has little military or monetary power, what source of influence is left to them? Every group of persons, no matter how poor or how powerless, can use integrity and moral suasion. The sages were a group of people who had little political power and certainly no military power. They could only persuade people of the rightness of their opinions and become leaders because of their fitness as role models of piety and integrity. (This is not very different from the situation of most rabbis today. Rabbis cannot really *make* people do anything, they can only convince people through personal example and teaching.)

Given these historical circumstances, it is not surprising, then, that the sages take a rather unique view of where power resides in human relationships. Power, for the sages, does not really rely on social standing, gender, might, or wealth. The person who has the power in a relationship is the person who has virtue on his or her side. Thus, as we shall see in the following accounts of what really goes on in marital relationships, the spouse who has virtue on his or her side is the person who is deemed to have the power.

We should sound one note of caution about these stories. Since the sages had a vested interest in seeing relationships in this way, they obviously would have tended to preserve stories that corroborated their point of view. No doubt in the sages' day, as in our own, there were plenty of people who felt that power was a function of money, social standing, physical might, or gender. What is interesting for our purposes is that, by and large, these are not the materials that have been preserved for us as expressions of the sages' Judaism.

Rachel and Rabbi Akiba

Of all the stories of marital devotion in rabbinic literature, the following is perhaps the most famous and best illustrates our basic thesis: the person with the power is not the one with money but the one with the vision. The three main characters in this tale are Ben Kalba Savua, one of the three richest men in Jerusalem of that day, his daughter Rachel, and a penniless shepherd named Akiba. Conventional thinking might lead us to believe that Ben Kalba Savua would be the most powerful of these three people, but our story shows us the opposite.

> Rabbi Akiba was a shepherd of Ben Kalba Savua. His [Ben Kalba Savua's] daughter saw how modest and noble

[the shepherd] was [and] said to him, "Were I to be betrothed to you, would you go away to [study at] the academy?" He said to her, "Yes." She was then secretly betrothed to him and sent him away. When her father heard [what she had done], he drove her from his house and forbade her by a vow to have any benefit from his estate.

[Rabbi Akiba] departed and spent twelve years at the academy. When he returned home he brought with him twelve thousand disciples. [While in his hometown] he heard an old man saying to her, "How long will you lead the life of living widowhood?" She said to him, "If he would listen to me he would spend [in study] another twelve years." Said [Rabbi Akiba], "It is then with her consent that I am acting," and he departed again and spent another twelve years at the academy. When he [finally] returned he brought with him twenty-four thousand disciples. His wife heard [of his arrival] and went out to meet him. Her neighbors said to her, "Borrow some [respectable] clothes and put them on." She said to them, "A righteous man regards the life of his beast" (Proverbs 12:10). On approaching him she fell upon her face and kissed his feet. His attendants were about to thrust her aside when [Rabbi Akiba] said to them, "Leave her alone, [what is] mine and yours are hers."

Her father heard that a great man had come to town and said "I shall go to him; it is possible he will invalidate my vow [against my daughter]." When he came to him, [Rabbi Akiba] said to him, "Would you have made your vow if you had known that he was a great man?" He said to him, "[Had he known] even one chapter or even one single *halakhah* [I would not have made the vow]." He then said to him, "I am the man." He fell upon his face and kissed his feet and also gave him half of his wealth. (B. *Ketubot* 62b–63a // B. *Nedarim* 50a)

Who has the power in this story? The most powerful person, as Rabbi Akiba readily admits, is Rachel. She has the strength to withstand poverty after having lived in luxury. She is clear eyed in her vision of what will be good for her (marrying Akiba) and good for her husband (sending him off to become a great scholar). All of Ben Kalba Savua's supposed power comes to naught when faced with his daughter's clear vision. Of course, we might also speculate that she was rebelling against a wealthy, powerful (and overbearing?) father by marrying an impoverished, illiterate shepherd. In the end, Ben Kalba Savua willingly admits defeat, wanting only to reestablish his relationship with his daughter. Thus, perfect symmetry is achieved in this legend: the illiterate, impoverished shepherd is, in the end, a learned, wealthy scholar because of the clear vision and moral power of his wife. It is Rachel, who is most in touch with God's will and willing to act on her insight, who has the most power in this story.

Beruriah and Rabbi Meir

Beruriah, like Rachel, demonstrated her moral authority over her husband, Rabbi Meir. In this passage, she also shows how cleverly she can interpret biblical verses.

> There were once some highwaymen in the neighborhood of Rabbi Meir who caused him a great deal of trouble. Rabbi Meir would [accordingly] pray that they should die. His wife Beruriah said to him: How do you make out [that such a prayer should be permitted]? Because it is written "Let chatta'im [sins] cease"? Is it written [let] chot'im [sinners] [cease]? It is written chatta'im [sins]! And further, look at the end of the verse: "and let the wicked

be no more" (Psalm 104:35). Since the sins will cease, there will be no more wicked men! Rather pray for them that they should repent, and [then] "the wicked will be no more." He did pray for them and they repented. (B. *Berakhot* 10a)

Obviously, Rabbi Meir was using as his prayer the following verse from Psalm 104:35: "Let sinners cease out of the earth, and let the wicked be no more." Apparently Rabbi Meir changed a vowel of one word in this verse or perhaps was inattentive to its literal meaning. Instead of saying *chata'aim*, which here means sinners but literally means sins, he apparently said *chot'im*, which can mean nothing *but* sinners. Beruriah then rebuked him and re-interpreted the verse using the literal meaning of the word *chata'aim* as it should be pronounced. Beruriah was able not only to correct Rabbi Meir's quotation of a biblical text and make it stick but she was also able to delve into the text's proper meaning and successfully rebuke her learned husband. In this story, she is literally and morally correct, and she is able to lead her husband to a correct prayer that solves his problem.

Imma Shalom and Rabbi Eliezer

Another famous sage's wife, Imma Shalom, also exercised some authority over her husband in what was probably a stormy marriage. She was caught between two sages— her husband Rabbi Eliezer and her brother, Rabban Gamaliel—who fought bitterly in the Academy. She tried her best to keep these two powerful men in her life from doing each other harm. In the following famous story, we learn how Rabbi Eliezer is finally excommunicated and forced from the Academy.

If he cut it [an oven made of many layers with sand between each layer into which an impure thing has fallen] into separate tiles, placing sand between each tile: Rabbi Eliezer declared it clean, and the sages declared it unclean; and this was the oven of 'Aknai. Why [the oven of] 'Aknai? Said Rav Judah in Samuel's name: [It means] that they encompassed it with arguments as a snake, and proved it unclean.

It has been taught: On that day Rabbi Eliezer brought forward every answer in the world, but they [the sages] did not accept them. Said he to them, "If the halakhah agrees with me, let this carob tree prove it!" Thereupon the carob tree was torn a hundred cubits out of its place (others say four hundred cubits). They said to him, "No proof can be brought from a carob tree."

Again he said to them, "If the halakhah agrees with me, let the stream of water prove it!" Whereupon the stream of water flowed backward. They said to him, "No proof can be brought from a stream of water."

Again he said to them, "If the halakhah agrees with me, let the walls of the schoolhouse prove it," whereupon the walls inclined to fall. But Rabbi Joshua rebuked them [the walls] and said to them, "When scholars are engaged in a halakhic dispute, what right have you to interfere?" Hence they did not fall, in honor of Rabbi Joshua, nor did they resume the upright, in honor of Rabbi Eliezer; and they are still standing thus inclined.

Again he said to them, "If the halakhah agrees with me, let it be proved from heaven!" Whereupon a Bat Kol (a Heavenly Voice) went forth and said, "Why do you [dispute] with Rabbi Eliezer, seeing that in all matters the halakhah agrees with him!" Rabbi Joshua arose and said, "It [the Torah] is not in heaven!" (Deuteronomy 30:12). What [did he mean by] "it is not in heaven"? Said Rabbi Jeremiah, "That the Torah had already been given at Mount Sinai; we pay no attention to a Heavenly Voice, because You have long since written in the Torah at Mount Sinai, 'After the majority one must incline'" (Exodus 23:2).

Rabbi Nathan met Elijah and said to him, "What did the Holy One, Blessed be He, do in that hour?" He laughed, saying, "My children have overcome me, My children have overcome me." They said, "On that day all objects that Rabbi Eliezer had declared clean were brought and burned in fire. Then they took a vote and excommunicated him." (B. *Bava Metsia* 59a–b)

This story only underscores the theme we are exploring in this chapter: not even scholarly acumen is more powerful than virtue (although they are closely matched). Pursuing one's own opinions, even if they are right, at the expense of the honor of a whole group of people is not virtuous behavior and ultimately does not succeed in the sages' system.

Rabbi Eliezer was so hurt by his excommunication, spearheaded by his brother-in-law Rabban Gamaliel, that he continued to bear a grudge against his wife's brother. Imma Shalom was apparently aware of this propensity in her husband to be resentful and took precautions against his violently expressing his hurt feelings.

Imma Shalom was Rabbi Eliezer's wife, and sister to Rabban Gamaliel. From the time of this incident onward she did not permit Rabbi Eliezer to fall upon his face. A certain day happened to be New Moon, and she mistook a full month for a defective one. Others say, a poor man came and stood at the door, and she took some bread to him. [On her return] she found him fallen on his face. She said to him, "Arise, you have slain my brother." In the meanwhile an announcement was made from the house of Rabban Gamaliel that he had died. He said to her, "Whence do you know it?" She said to him, "I have this tradition from my father's house: All gates are locked, excepting the gates of wounded feelings." (B. *Bava Metsia* 59b)

For quite some time after the excommunication, Imma Shalom did not allow her husband to fall on his face, that is, to make supplication to God regarding his hurt feelings. The issue involved with the New Moon is part of the complicated way the Jewish calendar was set. Jewish months are either 30 days long (a full month) or 29 days long (a "defective" month). If the previous month had been 30 days long, the 30th and 31st days would have been the New Moon, a semiholiday on which supplications about hurt feelings (*tachanun*) are not said. Imma Shalom apparently miscalculated and thought that the day on which this incident occurred was a New Moon. Therefore, she felt safe leaving her husband to his own devices. However, the previous month was actually 29 days long and the 31st day was not a semiholiday and *tachanun* could be said. An alternative tradition suggests that she simply wanted to perform the *mitsvah* of *tsedakah* (charity) when a beggar came to her door. For whatever reason, Imma Shalom left her husband alone for a few moments on a day when he could bring his case before God. When she found him in the position of supplication, she immediately recognized what he had done. She realized that his plea had been efficacious because of her father's teaching: God always listens to prayers about hurt feelings. Interestingly, she could quote this piece of wisdom as authoritatively as we suppose her brother might have done.

Rabbi Eliezer had a great deal of spiritual power. He was recognized as an authority in Jewish law who was a walking encyclopedia of knowledge, particularly about the way things had been done before the Temple was destroyed in 70 c.e. He was quite strict and, as we saw in this passage, utterly convinced of the correctness of his knowledge. In the sages' system he possessed a great deal of virtue, since learning was one of the things they held in highest esteem. However, Imma Shalom was able to exercise control over him through her understanding of virtue and fair play. It is ironic that the power of her virtuous watch over her husband may have been undone through her desire to perform the *mitsvah* of *tsedakah*. It seems somewhat more just that she simply might have miscalculated the date and Rabbi Eliezer, with his absolute knowledge of Jewish law, was able to take advantage of this error. The balance of power and virtue in this case is closely matched between Imma Shalom and her husband. We note that while a whole Academy of men was needed to control him when they argued on an intellectual basis alone, a single woman controlled him when she acted on the basis of mercy and concern for others.

Other Wives and Husbands

When the husband is not as spiritually powerful as was Rabbi Eliezer, a wife's virtue and generosity easily give her more power in their relationship.

R. Yose ben Saul told the story of the following case:
There was an incident involving a certain woman who
loved to perform the religious commandments [such as
feeding the hungry], while her husband hated to perform
them. Now a poor man came along, so she gave him food
and he ate. When she sensed that her husband was coming back, she took the poor man away and hid him in
the attic. She set food before her husband, and he ate
and then fell asleep. A snake came along and supped
from the same dish. When her husband woke up from
his sleep, he wanted to eat. The man in the attic began
to chatter [so warning the husband not to eat the food].
(Y. *Avodah Zarah* 2:3, 41a)

Clearly, this is a tale shaped to teach the merits of giving charity. However, it is interesting that whoever composed the story found it quite believable that a woman
could be more devoted to the *mitsvot* than her husband
and, seemingly, would overrule her husband in this matter and deceive him in order to perform *mitsvot*. Great
reward accrues to the man because of his wife's religious
devotion, a striking reversal of the usual portrayal of who
performs *mitsvot* for a family and who then benefits from
them. Usually, we think of the man performing *mitsvot*
and his family benefiting from them. Indeed, the roles of
the husband and wife in this story could easily have been
reversed, he being more devoted to doing *mitsvot* than
she. Perhaps the accretion of merit through *mitsvot* was
more of an egalitarian enterprise in the rabbinic era than
is generally believed.

Virtue can be wed to cleverness in order to subvert the
letter of the law when following the law would lead to heart-
ache. Though Jewish law states that a husband must divorce his wife after ten years of living together if they do

not have children, a woman was able to circumvent this law with the blessing of the sages.

Another explanation, "we will be glad and rejoice in you" (Song of Songs 1:4). We have learned elsewhere (M. *Yevamot* 6:6): If a man has married a wife and lived with her ten years and she has not borne him a child, he is not at liberty to neglect the duty [of begetting children]. Rabbi Idi said: It happened once that a woman in Sidon had lived ten years with her husband without bearing him a child. They came to R. Simeon ben Yochai and requested to be parted from one another. He said to them: I adjure you, just as you have always shared a festive board together, so do not part save with festivity. They took his advice and kept holiday and made a great feast and drank too much. Feeling then in a good humor he said to her: "My daughter, pick out any article you want in my house and take it with you to your father's house." What did she do? When he was asleep she gave an order to her servants and handmaids to lift him up on the bed and take and carry him to her father's house. At midnight he awoke from his sleep, and when the effects of the wine passed from him he said: "My daughter, where am I?" She said to him, "You are in my father's house." "And what am I doing in your father's house?" She said: "Did you not say to me last night, 'Take any article you like from my house and go to your father's house'? There is nothing in the world I care for more than you." They again went to Rabbi Simeon ben Yochai and he went and prayed for them and they became fertile. This shows that just as God makes barren women fertile, the righteous can make barren women fertile.

And is not the lesson clear: If a woman on saying to a mere mortal like herself, "There is nothing I care for more in the world than you" was visited, does it not stand to reason that Israel, who wait for the salvation of God every day and say, "We care for nothing in the world but You," will certainly be visited? Hence it is written, "we will be glad and rejoice in You." (*Song of Songs Rabbah* 1:4 ¶ 2)

Let us explain the last part of this passage first. The sages interpreted the love poetry of the Song of Songs in a metaphorical way. They saw the girl in the poems as Israel and the boy as God. The love poetry is therefore not an expression of adolescent passion but of the abiding relationship between Israel and God. Thus, this whole passage (Song of Songs 1:4) is a lesson to the Jewish people: if they will value God more highly than any material wealth, then God will grant Israel mercy and will look kindly on Israel's requests.

The neat way this story fits with this explanation of the verse and the highly romantic nature of the tale might naturally make us skeptical about its historicity. Nonetheless, what we can say is that it was plausible to those who composed this tale and to those who included it in this *Midrash* collection, that a woman could, through devotion to her husband, override the strict letter of the law through cleverly fulfilling her husband's words. Not only that, her actions are seen as meritorious and are rewarded. She, through genuine devotion (and quick thinking), demonstrates that virtue which, to the sages' way of thinking, is the real source of power in relationships.

Laypeople Have More Virtue than Sages . . .

If we are suggesting that power in a marital relationship resides with that person who behaves most righteously, then we must also be prepared to demonstrate the opposite: those who do not behave righteously lack power in relationships. In what may be our most fascinating passage on the subject, we learn that the sages were more troubled by their *yetser hara*, their inclination to do evil (mostly, the urge to have sexual intercourse), than any other group of people.

> Abaye said, Against scholars more than anyone else [does the evil inclination act]; as was the case when Abaye heard a certain man saying to a certain woman, "Let us arise betimes and go on our way." Said [Abaye], "I will follow them in order to keep them away from transgression," and he followed them for three *parasangs* across the meadows. When they parted company he heard them say, "Our company is pleasant, the way is long." Said Abaye, "If it were I, I could not have restrained myself," and so he went and leaned in deep anguish against a doorpost, when a certain old man [i.e., Elijah] came up to him and taught him: The greater the man, the greater his evil inclination. (B. *Sukkah* 52a)

Abaye apparently trailed this couple for quite a distance. A *parasang* is roughly 2.5 miles, so he followed this couple for some 8 miles. He was sure that in that space of time, isolated in meadows, they would commit some sin. However, they did not do so and Abaye marveled at their self-restraint while experiencing a loss of self-esteem as he realized his own weakness. This story illustrates a well-known truth: intellectual acumen and a dynamic personality are not necessarily connected to moral stature or restraint. The anonymous man and woman are straw figures in this story, but their behavior seems plausible. They are simply seeking companionship and perhaps safety as they travel some distance from one place to another. They are the powerful ones in this story and Abaye is weak. Note that the anonymous man and woman are equal in their power: their virtue transcends gender.

The stories about relationships between men and women in rabbinic literature tend to be dramatic and to highlight extremes of devotion or faithlessness. This is for the obvious reason that such stories can be used to illustrate moral precepts and also for the same reason that "Man Bites Dog" is worthy of a headline while "Dog Bites Man" is not: one is more remarkable than the other. In the normal scheme of things, great numbers of men and women probably walked together, worked together, and lived together without the "evil urge" overcoming them. However, this is not exceptional behavior and therefore is probably not reported on in proportion to the frequency with which it occurred. That makes this story all the more important since it gives us a tiny glimpse of the average, everyday, undramatic lives that men and women may have lived in the rabbinic era.

. . . Sometimes

However, when the sages wish to tell a tale of faithlessness and faithfulness, they do so with a literary flair that underscores our theme: virtue triumphs in the end. In this case, a most unfaithful wife, and a most faithful one, are contrasted.

A certain man heard his wife say to her daughter, Why do you not observe more secrecy in your amours? I have ten children and only one is from your father. When [the man] lay [on his deathbed], he said to them [his family], I leave all my property to one son. They did not know which of them he meant, so they consulted Rabbi Bana'ah. He said to them: Go and knock on the grave of your father, until he gets up and reveals to you which one of you [he has made his heir]. So they all went to do so. The one who was really his son did not go. He [Rabbi Bana'ah thereupon] said to them: All the estate belongs to this one. They then went and slandered him [Rabbi Bana'ah] before the king saying: There is a man among the Jews who extorts money from people without witnesses or anything else. So they took him and they threw him in prison.

His wife came [to the court] and said to them: I had a slave, and some men have cut off his head, skinned him, eaten the flesh and filled the skin with water and given students to drink from it, and they have not paid me either its price or its hire. They did not know what to make of what she had said to them, so they said: Let us fetch the wise man of the Jews and he will tell us. So they called Rabbi Bana'ah and he said to them: She means a goat skin bottle. Since he is so wise let him sit in the gate and act as a judge. (B. *Bava Batra* 58a)

First of all, we have in this story a patently unfaithful wife whose daughter is apparently following in her mother's footsteps—and her mother is encouraging her! The woman's husband then seeks to leave his fortune to his only biologic son and Rabbi Bana'ah cleverly tricks the children into revealing which is the true heir by suggesting that they treat their father's grave in an undignified manner. The greedy children are obviously chagrined and have Rabbi Bana'ah thrown in jail. Here is the low point of the story, where unfaithfulness and avarice have brought the pro-

tagonist. Next, a faithful—and clever—wife will bring him
back to honor. She poses a riddle to the court that they
cannot decipher. They must fetch Rabbi Bana'ah from
prison to solve the puzzle and he is reinstated as a judge.
Here we have a balanced picture of women's roles in
marriage. Women can be faithless or faithful; stupidly
duplicitous (as is the wanton wife) or clever and true (as
is Rabbi Bana'ah's wife). Indeed, Rabbi Bana'ah's wife is
portrayed as his partner and equal in terms of tricking
people into doing the right thing. Underlying all these
machinations is the concept that the virtuous party in the
relationships triumphs. The cuckolded husband is able to
leave his estate to his one biologic son and Rabbi
Bana'ah's wife succeeds in having her husband released
from jail.

We do find accounts in our literature of women who may
have been unfaithful, which are not paired with stories of
faithful wives. For example, we have a long passage at
the end of a tractate that strings together many examples
of possibly wanton wives. These examples are brought
in connection with M. *Nedarim* 11:12. This mishnah
raises the issue of an unfaithful woman who, in former
times, was to be divorced simply by claiming to have been
unfaithful but who must now bring proof of her unfaithfulness before being divorced. Of course, the faithfulness
of husband and wife is related metaphorically to the theme
of this entire tractate—the keeping of vows and ways to
annul them when necessary—and the tractate may close
with this material as a way of summarizing, or encapsu-
lating, those themes.

Every day a certain woman would rise [in the morning]
and wash her husband's hands whenever intimacy had

taken place. One day she brought him water to wash. He said to her, "But nothing has taken place today!" She said, "If so, [it must have been] one of the gentile soap sellers who were here now; if not you, perhaps it was one of them." Said Rav Nachman: [We fear that] she conceived a passion for another, and her declaration has no substance.

A certain woman showed displeasure with her husband. Said he to her, "Why this change now? [Why are you angry today?]" She said to him, "You have never caused me so much pain through intimacy as today [and therefore I am angry with you]." He said, "But there has been none today!" She said, "If so, [it must have been] the gentile naphtha sellers who were here today; if not you, perhaps it was one of them." Said Rav Nachman to them: Disregard her; she has conceived a passion for another.

A certain man was closeted in a house with a [married] woman. [Hearing] the master [her husband] entering, the adulterer broke through a hedge and fled. Said Rava: The wife is permitted to her husband; had he committed the wrong, he would have hidden himself [in the house].

A certain adulterer visited a woman. Her husband came, whereupon the lover went and placed himself behind a curtain before the door. Now, some cress was lying there, and a snake [came and ate] thereof; the master [her husband] was about to eat of the cress, unknown to his wife. He [the lover] said to him [the husband], "Do not eat it because a snake has tasted it." Said Rava: the wife is permitted: had he committed wrong, he would have been pleased that he should eat thereof and die, as it is written, "For they have committed adultery and blood is in their hands" (Ezekiel 23:37). Surely that is obvious?— I might think that he had committed wrong, and as for his warning, that is because he prefers the husband not to die, so that his wife may be to him as "stolen waters are sweet and bread eaten in secret is pleasant" (Proverbs 9:17). Therefore he teaches otherwise [i.e., the lover behaved decently in respect to adultery and saving the husband's life]. (B. *Nedarim* 91b)

We have here four case histories that two authorities, Rav Nachman and Rava, rule on. In the first case, the woman indicates that she has slept with someone other than her husband. In former times, according to the mishnah, she would have been divorced. However, Rav Nachman rules that she has simply fallen in love with someone other than her husband and made the statement in order to obtain a divorce and that, therefore, her statement is ignored. The second example follows a similar line of reasoning. In the first case involving Rava, an adulterer hears his (alleged) lover's husband enter the house and noisily flees. Rava rules that adultery must not have taken place or he would not have left so noisily, hence the woman is not divorced. Similarly, in the last case, Rava rules that no adultery took place because the adulterer warns the husband about possible poison in his food and saves the husband's life, and it is more likely that, had he been the woman's lover, the adulterer would have wanted to see the husband dead. As proof, Rava cites the verse from Ezekiel that links adultery and murder. In other words, if someone does not hesitate to commit adultery they would not hesitate to commit murder, either. Therefore, a man who would not commit murder, or allow a man's death, is not suspected of adultery. An objection to this teaching is then raised. Perhaps the adulterer wants the husband to stay alive; that is, he is more interested in adultery than in sex that could be legally sanctioned. However, this objection is rejected. The conclusion is that the possible adulterer acted decently throughout the episode.

We note that all four of these rulings have the effect of preserving the marriages in question. It appears that the first two women may have been attempting to manipulate the law in order to force their husbands to grant them divorces because they have apparently fallen in love with other men. Who has the power in this situation? The spouse who wants to continue the marriage or the spouse who is no longer faithful (at least psychologically)? The sages rule on the side of the existing relationship, perhaps hoping to discourage unfaithful behavior by not rewarding it. In these cases, as in all those we have seen in the relationship between a woman and a man, virtue is power.

Does virtue lead to power today in personal relationships? Yes, it does, although this may not seem to be the case, especially during a divorce. However, it is generally true that in human relations the person who acts with the most *menschlichkeit* hurts the most in the short run and the least in the long run. Conversely, the person who behaves with the least integrity in a situation appears to "get away with it" for a while but ends up hurting the most in the long run. So the sages' insights still hold true: virtue is power.

5

Virtue as Power II: Women and Power in Society

Women, Virtue, and Power

I doubt there are many among us who can forget the following image from the uprising of students in Tiananmen Square in China in 1989. A column of tanks was brought to a stop by a lone man, carrying his shopping bags, who refused to move. He stood there, alone and unarmed, in front of a tank and, through his courage and belief, made it stop. Before that encounter, one might have thought that a single person could not wield influence over a tank. And yet, the standoff became a graphic illustration of the power of courage, faith, and virtue over brute force.

We are accustomed to thinking of men in the rabbinic era as the group of persons with authority over learning, money, and politics—in short, a group with power. However, as with any stereotype, while there is some truth to this image, it is also incomplete. When we examine our sources, we find that women wielded quite a bit of power. As in male–female relationships, the source of power for persons of either gender in their dealings with society is their virtue. In other words, since virtue and Torah were intimately connected for the sages, and since the sages recognized that Torah transcends gender, it logically follows that power based on virtue also transcends gender. And this is what we find in the following cases and stories. Women wield the power that stems from virtue and women who lack virtue cannot wield power.

Rabbi's Maid

We have two instances in which Rabbi's maid exercises authority and power. She is one of our least likely prospects to be a powerful person: a servant and a woman. Yet, as we see in these two passages, she is able to pronounce moral judgment on others. Not only does she use the sages' technique of backing up her judgment with a verse from the Torah, she is capable of influencing the sages' behavior.

In general, the sages interpreted the verse, "Do not put a stumbling block before the blind" (Leviticus 19:14) metaphorically. They took this as a general injunction not to "trip up" any person in their "blind spot." So, in their minds, this verse forbids us to offer wine to someone who has taken a vow not to drink wine (B. *Avodah Zarah* 6a), lend money without witnesses, since this tempts the borrower to simply abscond with the money (B. *Bava Metsia* 75b), or tear up an expensive piece of clothing in front of people just to see whether they'll fly into a rage (B. *Kiddushin* 32a). Rabbi's maid, understanding the way the sages interpret this verse, extends this basic interpretation to another situation.

> When Rabbi's maid saw a man beating his grown-up son, she said, "That man should be placed under a ban for he is violating, 'Do not put a stumbling block before the blind'" (Leviticus 19:14). (B. *Mo'ed Katan* 17a // Y. *Mo'ed Katan* 3:1)

We learn in the Torah that a child who strikes his or her parent is subject to the death penalty (Exodus 21:15). Therefore, when Rabbi's maid sees a man beating his grown-up son she chastises the father for "putting a stumbling block" before the son. In this case, the father is tempting the grown son to hit him back, thereby incurring the death penalty. Not only did Rabbi's maid generate a valid new interpretation of Leviticus 19:14 but her ban was actually carried out! Again, we see our basic principle in action: Torah and virtue transcend gender and imbue those who have internalized them with power regardless of their gender and worldly status.

Rabbi's maid's less-official injunctions were also heeded by the scholars who frequented Rabbi's house. Apparently, Rabbi's maid expressed herself in a somewhat idiosyncratic way called "enigmatic speech." Interestingly, the phrase in Hebrew for "enigmatic speech" is *l'shon chokhmah*, "the language of wisdom." The following is but one example of this "language of wisdom."

> When Rabbi's maid indulged in enigmatic speech she used to say this: "The ladle strikes against the jar, let the eagles fly to their nests. [The students may now leave the dining room for their lodgings.]" And when she wished them to remain at table she used to tell them, "The crown

of her friend shall be removed and the ladle will float in the jar like a ship that sails in the sea." (B. *Eruvin* 53b)

Apparently, when Rabbi's maid felt that the students of the sages had spent enough time at Rabbi's dining, she would urge them to fly like eagles to their nests and when she wished to urge them to stay she would make her latter statement. There is some thought that this was her delicate way of saying either, "There's no more wine for the ladle to dish out" or "There is yet wine left for the ladle to dish out." Apparently her hints were heeded and learning her particular use of language was possibly part of the informal initiation into the sages' culture. Though Rabbi was a great scholar and teacher, his maid, too, obviously wielded power over the sages who gathered at his home. While she may have had no formal standing as a sage, it is clear that she absorbed quite a bit of the sages' learning and that this learning was respected. Indeed, her judgments carried weight in the sages' world regardless of her low social standing, her gender, and her anonymity. (We are given no hint of her actual name.) In fact, as we shall see in the chapter on loss, Rabbi's maid can even overrule all the sages together.

Helene

A woman who enjoyed a more conventional sort of power was Helene. Helene lived in the first century C.E. and was the sister and wife of Munbaz I, king of Adiabene. Helene and her son Izates converted to Judaism in about 30 C.E. through the influence of Ananias, a Jewish merchant. Helene spent the latter part of her life in Jerusalem, where she built a palace. She died in Adiabene, but her remains were buried in Jerusalem in the Tomb of the Kings.

Helene is portrayed in rabbinic literature as exercising power both as it is conventionally understood and also the power associated with virtue. For example, she is remembered for making lavish donations to the Temple.

Helene his [Munbaz the king's] mother made a candelabra of gold over the entrance of the Sanctuary and she also made a tablet of gold with the *sotah* portion on it (Numbers 5:11–31). (M. *Yoma* 3:10)

The candelabra that Helene put on the Sanctuary was placed at the very top of the building so that, at sunrise, it would glitter and the inhabitants of Jerusalem could tell it was time to recite the morning *Shema*, which is to be said at sunrise (T. *Yoma* 2:3). The scroll with the *sotah* portion refers to that passage in the Torah concerning a woman who is suspected of adultery. This passage from the Torah is written down and combined with bitter waters and the suspected adulteress drinks it in order to determine if she has actually been unfaithful. This golden version of it was made so that, when it was needed, no one would have to hunt for a Torah scroll but rather could sit in front of this tablet and copy the passage down.

This mishnah is one of three mishnayot (M. *Yoma* 3:9–11) that contrast those who are remembered with praise and those who are remembered in shame for their contributions to the Temple or their lack thereof. Those who contributed lavish, or simply practical, improvements to the Temple are remembered with praise. Those who had special skills in preparing materials for the Temple, or in singing or writing, and who refused to teach these skills to others were remembered for shame. Helene is the only woman in either group.

In addition, we note that all the other contributions listed have to do specifically with the functioning of the Temple, particularly on Yom Kippur. Helene's gifts relate much more to the common person and the performance of basic *mitsvot*. In fact, her gifts seem aimed, first, at maintaining people's relationships with God by reminding them to say the *Shema* and, second, maintaining people's relationships with each other through the use of the *sotah* passage. It is tempting to suspect that this represents the different interests of men and women in their charitable pursuits.

Today, we find that women use the power of their philanthropy to further those causes that are meaningful to them and give money to charitable causes for different reasons than do men. For example, women seem to be much more interested in the end result of their philanthropy than in the secondary gain they experience from belonging to an organization such as, for example, the Major Contributors Circle of a Federation.[1] Could Helene be an early forerunner of these independent, grass-roots-oriented, feminist philanthropists? It is tempting to propose such a theory, but we are obviously on weak historical ground when we make such a suggestion. Still, it is food for thought.

Helene's power does not stem only from her wealth. She is portrayed as being quite punctilious in her observance of the *mitsvot*. For example, the *Mishnah* teaches that she went beyond the letter of the law in her spiritual devotion to Judaism by taking Nazirite vows. The biblical basis for this institution is Numbers 6:1–21. These vows, taken for limited periods of time by men and women alike,

entailed three duties above and beyond the normal observance of *mitsvot*: not cutting one's hair for the dura-
tion of the vow (this was Samson's undoing since he was
a special type of Nazirite for life), not drinking wine or
liquor, and avoiding contact with dead bodies and the
ritual impurity associated with them. If a person trans-
gressed these principles before the period of the vow was
over, he or she had to go through a purification ritual and
start the full period of observance over again. After the
Temple was destroyed no one took Nazirite vows. One
other fact we should know before we study this mishnah
is that the countries outside the Land of Israel were considered ritually impure and so Nazirite vows could only
be correctly observed in the Land of Israel.

> One who made a vow for a prolonged period and com-
> pleted his period of being a Nazirite and afterward came
> to the Land [of Israel], Beit Shammai say, He must con-
> tinue as a Nazirite for thirty days. And Beit Hillel say, He
> must be a Nazirite from the beginning [i.e., all over again].
> It once happened that Helene the queen's son went to
> war and she said, "If my son will come [back] safely from
> the war I will be a Nazirite for seven years." And her son
> came back from the war [safely] and she was a Nazirite
> for seven years. And at the end of seven years she went
> up to the Land [of Israel] and Beit Hillel adjured her that
> she be a Nazirite for another seven years. And at the end
> of seven years she became unclean and she turned out
> to be a Nazir for twenty-one years. Said Rabbi Judah, "She
> was a Nazir for only fourteen years." (M. *Nazir* 3:6)

What happened here? Helene took a vow to observe
this self-dedicated form of Judaism if her son survived the
war. He returned safely and she observed the Nazirite rules

for seven years. (Apparently, people became Nazirites outside the Land of Israel even though these countries were considered ritually impure.) However, at the end of that time she came to the Land of Israel which, in effect, invalidated the seven years she had already observed these rules and she had to abide by them for yet another seven years in the purity of the Land of Israel. Then, at the very end of this second seven-year period, she became ritually impure and here we have a difference of opinion. Some say that she observed yet another full seven years of Nazirite rules. Rabbi Judah says she added only thirty days extra to compensate for the impurity she experienced at the end of her second seven years and so observed the Nazirite rules for a total of fourteen years and thirty days. In any case, Helene is held up here as a model of observance of this special, rigorous form of Jewish devotion.

Her observance of more conventional *mitsvot* was exemplary, as well. As befits a woman of her wealth, she apparently had a huge sukkah; so huge, in fact, that the sages question whether it was perhaps a touch *too* large to qualify as a humble, temporary dwelling.

> "A *sukkah* that is taller than twenty cubits is invalid" (M. *Sukkah* 1:1). R. Judah declares it valid. Said R. Judah: Helene's *sukkah* was twenty cubits tall and the sages went in and out, when visiting her, and they did not say a thing. They said to him, It was because she is a woman and a woman is not liable to keep the commandment of dwelling in a *sukkah*. He said to them, Now did she not have seven sons who are disciples of sages, and all of them were dwelling in [that same *sukkah*]! (T. *Sukkah* 1:1)

Why should a *sukkah* taller than twenty cubits (about thirty-five feet) be invalid? Various authorities suggest different answers. It might be because the sages considered that any structure over twenty cubits high would entail so much labor and material that it would be permanent and the *sukkah* must be a temporary structure. Others suggest that, with a roof this high, one would be sitting under the shade of the walls rather than the shade of the *sekhakh*, the roofing of vegetation, as required. The *Yerushalmi* (*Sukkah* 1:1, 51d) suggests that it may have been because the sides did not reach all the way to the top of the *sukkah*. Apparently, wealthy *sukkah* builders often left a space between the top of the *sukkah* wall and the roof so that air might pass through the sukkah and cool it off, which is not the way a *sukkah* ought to be built.

It appears from this story that Helene had a magnificent *sukkah* that reached the limits of permissible height (and the *Bavli* [B. *Sukkah* 2b] suggests higher than that) and that the sages visited it with pleasure. There seems to be some confusion as to whether this *sukkah* was too high or was invalidated in some other way. If it was invalid, how then did the sages justify dwelling in it? At first they suggested that since she was a woman, and as such exempt from positive time-bound commandments, she need not have built her *sukkah* correctly. However, this argument was refuted by the assertion that she had seven sons who were students of the sages and they *were* obligated to observe this commandment correctly and thus seemed to validate Helene's *sukkah* as kosher. The *Bavli* (B. *Sukkah* 2b–3a) suggests that the problem with Helene's *sukkah* was not its height but the fact that it had many recesses in it and that her sons dwelt in one area that was clearly large enough by itself to be a kosher *sukkah* while Helene, out of modesty, dwelt in a smaller recess by herself that might have been too small to be considered a valid *sukkah* on its own.

There seems to be some confusion over exactly what was questionable about Helene's *sukkah*, although the general picture is clear: she had an absolutely magnificent *sukkah* that the sages considered valid even though it bordered on the invalid. This might have been a problem for a person less well known for her observance of the *mitsvot* according to the sages' rulings. Likewise, a person with less wealth than Helene who built such a *sukkah* might be seen as building an addition to his or her house rather than merely constructing a temporary dwelling for the holiday. However, the sages recognized that Helene was building a *sukkah* that befit her station in life and her custom of observing of the *mitsvot* in as lavish a manner as possible. This is consistent with her other acts of generosity, for she apparently used her sizable *sukkah* to entertain the sages and they evidently relished the opportunity to observe the holiday in a luxurious manner.

This generosity of hers, and her use of wealth for the public good is seen, in a veiled way, in yet another passage. In the year 45 c.e., famine struck Israel and Helene bought grain and figs in Egypt and Cyprus for the starving people.[2] However, as the following passage shows, she was not given the credit for this fine deed.

It is related of Munbaz the king that he stood and dissipated all his treasures to the poor in years of scarcity. His brothers sent to him and said to him, "Your father saved up treasures and added to the treasures of his fathers, and you are squandering what is yours and your fathers'." He said to them: My fathers stored up below and I am storing up above, as it says, "Truth springs out of the earth and righteousness [*tsedeq*] looks down from heaven" (Psalm 85:12). My father stored in a place that can be tampered with, but I have stored in a place that cannot be tampered with as it says, "Righteousness [*tsedeq*] and judgment are the foundation of his throne" (Psalm 97:2). My fathers stored up something that produces no fruits, but I have stored something that does produce fruits, as it is written, "Say you of the righteous [*tsaddiq*] that it shall be well with them, for they shall eat of the fruit of their doings" (Isaiah 3:10). My fathers gathered treasures of money, but I have gathered treasures of souls, as it is written, "The fruit of the righteous [*tsaddiq*] is the tree of life, and he that is wise wins souls" (Proverbs 11:30). My fathers gathered for others and I have gathered for myself, as it says, "And for you it shall be righteousness [*tsedaqah*]" (Deuteronomy 24:13). My fathers gathered for this world, but I have gathered for the future world, as it says, "Your righteousness [*tsidqecha*] shall go before you and the glory of the Lord shall go by your rearguard" (Isaiah 58:8). (T. *Pe'ah* 4:18 // Y. *Pe'ah* 1:1, 15b–c // B. *Bava Batra* 11a)

This passage is part of a beautiful, extended *nechemta*, that is, a comforting, uplifting message, about charity at the end of tractate T. *Pe'ah*. It is an extended exposition on the merits of charity that interweaves proof texts containing forms of the root *tsadi-dalet-quf* that has to do with charity, righteousness, and justice. This is an inspiring and impressive literary passage. But what is most interesting for our purposes is that Helene's deeds are attributed to Munbaz, her husband. Which source is more historically accurate here—Josephus, a Jewish historian who credits Helene with this generous act, or *Tosefta*, which gives the credit to her husband? It would be difficult for us to know for a certainty, at a remove of two thousand years. However, this act of generosity is certainly consistent with what else we know about Helene. Her other acts of philanthropy involved the grand and generous performance of *mitsvot* that involved average, everyday Jews. Saving people from starvation definitely fits with her character as we know it.

Helene may, in fact, be an example par excellence of a woman who wielded power based not only on virtue but on the more conventional basis of power—wealth—as well. Certainly, there were other wealthy women living in Israel during this period (e.g., Martha; see the chapter on entering and exiting relationships). However, Martha is not portrayed positively as a powerful woman because the sages did not perceive her wealth and her power to be allied with virtue. In fact, as we shall see in the chapter on loss, the sages portray her wealth as ultimately having no saving power. Helene, on the other hand, is seen as powerful not because of her wealth alone, but because that wealth is used to serve virtuous ends.

A Woman in Court

One could exercise power without the benefits of proximity to the sages, which Rabbi's maid had, or wealth, which Helene had. All one needed to have was a knowledge of the upright course of action in order to be heeded and wield power. For example, one woman who comes to court is able to use her knowledge of the law in what ends up to be her advantage.

Rabban Simeon b. Gamaliel says, "Any wound for which there is a fixed cost for healing it [she is healed at the expense of] her marriage contract. And [any wound] for which there is no fixed cost of healing—she is healed from [her husband's] support" (T. *Ketubot* 4:5). There is a relevant case. A [wounded or sick] woman came to Rabbi Jochanan. He said to her, "If there is a fixed fee [for healing], you will lose out." She said to him, "No. [There is no fixed fee.]" [She said to him further,] "Did not Rabbi Chaggai say in the name of Rabbi Joshua ben Levi, 'Do not be like lawyers, for you should not reveal to an individual the law [governing his case]?'" He knew that she was a proper person [and would not lie, e.g., claiming that there was no fixed fee demanded by the physician, if there actually was one]. (Y. *Ketubot* 4:11, 29a // Y. *Bava Batra* 9:4)

Here we have an example of a woman who, by demonstrating her knowledge of the law, earns the trust of the judge and a judgment in her favor. The principle involved here is that a husband must provide his wife with food, clothing, and marital relations. There is obviously no fixed amount of money a man must spend on food for his wife: it is an unlimited amount of money. Rabban Simeon ben Gamaliel likens healing that has no fixed price to this obligation to provide food, which has no price limit, and makes it part of a husband's obligation to his wife. However, if there is a fixed amount of money required for healing, then the sum comes out of the wife's *ketubah*, that is, that money that she brought to the marriage and that she would take from the marriage, in addition to what her husband guaranteed her, if she were to be divorced. Therefore, it is to the woman's advantage for there *not* to be a fixed price for the physician's services. Rabbi Jochanan hints at this principle to the woman who has come before him. She then rebukes him for acting improperly, since a judge should not also act as an advocate, which Rabbi Jochanan does here by hinting at what she should say so that the judgment would turn out to her advantage. When he hears her quoting a sage's words stating that this is not proper judicial procedure he realizes (a) that she knows the law and doesn't need it to be told to her and (b) since she is telling him not to do something improper that she is an honest person and is telling the truth: there was no fixed fee for the healing and her husband must pay for it. This woman's wisdom and honesty equal power in the sages' world.

A Woman and Her Bequest

A woman and her family can even overcome a sage's power when they are practicing their Judaism in good faith and when the sage in question may be holding too strictly to his own individual views. The sage in question here is Rabbi Eliezer, Imma Shalom's husband, who, as we already saw, was extremely knowledgeable but very stubborn in trying to force others to adhere to his individual version of the law. The woman, who is known only as the mother of the sons of Rochel, transferred property in a way that did not conform to Rabbi Eliezer's dictates. He felt that one should not distribute property by word of mouth. In other words, if we want to leave an item to someone after our death, we must give it to them outright rather than simply saying, "You may have X after I die." However, this woman does transfer a valuable piece of property in this way and is permitted by other sages to do so.

> It once happened that the mother of the sons of Rochel
> was ill and said, "Give my brooch, which is worth twelve
> *manehs*, to my daughter." She died and they fulfilled her
> words. He [Rabbi Eliezer] said to them, "The sons of
> Rochel! Their mother ought to have buried them."
> (M. *Bava Batra* 9:7)

This brooch must have been quite expensive since a
maneh is the highest value of coin in the rabbinic system. Therefore, transferring it to her daughter meant that
the mother was depriving her sons of a great deal of their
inheritance, which she was entitled to do. Her transfer to
her daughter, even though not accomplished according
to the *Mishnah*'s rules, is considered valid by her sons
who carry out her bequest and they are cursed by Rabbi
Eliezer for their action.

Why would Rabbi Eliezer curse sons for honoring a
mother's bequest, particularly when they stand to lose
economically by doing so? It would seem the height of
meritorious behavior. Apparently, these sons had a reputation for not following all of Rabbi Eliezer's rulings and
this gained them an evil reputation, at least with Rabbi
Eliezer. Our sources (Y. *Bava Batra* 9:7, 17b and B. *Bava
Batra* 156b) define their wickedness as growing two spe-
cies of plants together in a vineyard, which is forbidden;
in this case, grapes together with thistles or saffron. In
M. *Kilayim* 5:8, Rabbi Eliezer rules that such planting is
forbidden. In the case of the brooch, however, it is Rabbi
Eliezer's individual opinion that the mother of the sons of
Rochel transgresses by transferring her property with
words rather than through physical transferal. These circumstances suggest that her family may simply have
followed customs that differed from those of Rabbi Eliezer.

Who wins in this situation? The sage who is recognized as a brilliant teacher of authoritative positions but who is inflexible in his administration of his views? Or the woman who was apparently making a simple bequest without following all the technicalities of the law and her children who honored this bequest? Virtue is power. The family's actions are considered valid and the bequest is allowed to take place. This is quite striking since we would imagine that learning overcomes virtue, but that is clearly not what is happening in this case. Learning and virtue must be allied. Learning by itself does not yield power.

Virtue and Political Power

The sages' attitudes toward power were not universally held, as we can see in the following passage:

> Our rabbis taught: [If a nursing mother] gave her child to a wet nurse or weaned him, or he died, she is permitted to marry again forthwith. Rav Papa and Rav Huna, son of Rav Joshua, intended to give a practical decision in accordance with this teaching, [but] an aged woman said to them, "I have been in such a position and Rav Nachman forbade me [to marry again]." Surely, this could not have been so; for has not Rav Nachman in fact permitted [such remarriage] in the Exilarch's family?— The family of the Exilarch was different [from ordinary people] because no nurse would break her agreement with them. (B. *Ketubot* 60b)

We need to know about the role of nursing and the status of the Exilarch for this passage to make sense. Nursing was far more crucial to a child's development then than it is now. Now, if a woman wishes to formula feed her child, she may do so. The child's survival does not depend on her ability to nurse or find a wet nurse. However, in the sages' day this was not the case: a woman was obligated to nurse her child for a minimum of two years or had to provide a wet nurse for this purpose. The sages instituted several rulings to protect a woman's milk supply, one of which was a prohibition against remarriage for a woman who was widowed or divorced during the child's first two years of life, since the sages assumed a pregnancy would quickly ensue after such a marriage and thereby reduce the child's milk supply, endangering the child's life. However, if this widowed or divorced woman had engaged a wet nurse, one ruling states that she is permitted to remarry since the child will have a steady milk supply from this wet nurse. Then we learn that a woman who had been in such a position, that is, wishing to remarry during her child's first two years of life and having hired a wet nurse for the child, was forbidden to marry. This woman's citing of Rav Nachman's ruling is believed, although a contradictory ruling of his is also cited.

Why would Rav Nachman rule one way in one case and another way in a very similar case? Rav Nachman was well acquainted with the power of the Exilarch's family, since his father-in-law held this position. The Exilarch was part of the aristocracy and was quite powerful politically. Being hired by this family would be like being hired by the governor of a state: one would not break a contract with such a person lightly. Therefore, Rav Nachman had great confidence that the wet nurse for this child would work the whole two years and so allowed the child's mother to remarry. Rav Nachman's two views are thus reconciled. The basic issue is that the child's nutrition is assured. If it can be ascertained that this is the case, then there is no logical basis for preventing the mother's re-marriage.

What is really interesting for us is that the old woman's experience and testimony are validated. She, like a disciple of a sage, can validly pass on Rav Nachman's teaching, even when it contradicts another, perhaps better known, ruling of his. This, in the sages' system, is power: the ability to authoritatively quote learning and shape rulings by it. This anonymous woman's experience is validated and she is given as much power as any man in terms of her ability to pass a teaching on and be heard.

Yalta and Rav Nachman

In the last passage we examined, we saw that the sages' ideas about power were not the only ones that operated in the world. Clearly, more conventional definitions of power, such as political clout, were also operative and occasionally clashed with the sages' ideas about where power lay. Yalta, Rav Nachman's wife, provides us with an example of how her considerable power, stemming from her father's position as Exilarch in Babylonia, could be overcome by a sage's power, even when that sage would appear to have much less power than she does. The sage in this case is Ulla, an unordained but distinguished teacher from the Land of Israel.

Ulla happened to be at the house of Rav Nachman. They had a meal and he said grace and he handed the cup of benediction to Rav Nachman. Rav Nachman said to him: Please send the cup of benediction to Yalta. He said to him: Thus said Rabbi Jochanan: The fruit of a woman's body is not blessed unless from the fruit of a man's body, since it says, "He will also bless the fruit of your body" (Deuteronomy 7:13). It does not say the fruit of *her* body but the fruit of *your* body. . . . Meanwhile Yalta heard [that Ulla refused to send her a cup] and she got up in a passion and went to the wine store and broke four hundred jars of wine. Rav Nachman said to him: Let the Master send her another cup. He sent it to her with a message: All that wine can be counted as a benediction [i.e., she need not drink directly from the cup of benediction]. She returned answer: Gossip comes from peddlers and vermin from rags (*mimahadurei milei umismartutei kalmei*). (B. *Berakhot* 51b)

The grace after meals, *birkat hamazon*, was said over a cup of wine. Apparently, Yalta was used to participating fully in this ritual and became insulted when Ulla suggested that the cup her husband drank sufficed for her as well. Indeed, this practice is the subject of discussion in the *Bavli*, for some authorities believe the cup must be shared with the members of the household and some do not require this. At any rate, Ulla's refusal to send her the cup threw her into a destructive rage (although the claim of four hundred broken jars of wine is doubtless an exaggeration). Rav Nachman, probably knowing his wife's temper and predictable reaction to such a slight, urges Ulla to give his wife some of the wine of benediction. Ulla continues to refuse, saying that any of the wine from the broken jars will suffice since the wine for grace need not be drunk directly out of the cup of benediction. Hearing this, Yalta tacitly admits defeat by dispatching Ulla with a rhymed, insulting epithet. She likens Ulla's teachings to gossip from peddlers (a low class in her eyes) and denigrates the fact that he comes from Israel. In other words, one would expect vermin to issue forth from rags and she expects a second-rate sage to come from the Land of Israel since Babylonia was, in her mind at least, the center of learning at that time.

This scenario is somewhat reminiscent of a wealthy, powerful woman who is a member of her synagogue's board in a large metropolitan area. She may ask her rabbi, who hails from a small town, to do something the rabbi doesn't feel is correct. When the rabbi refuses, she may throw her weight around but eventually capitulate, saying something like, "If you lay down with a dog you'll get up with fleas."

Ulla and Yalta were well matched opponents. He was known for his strict rulings on questions of Jewish law (B. *Shabbat* 147a) and was capable of making insulting comments about those sages whose rulings he disliked (e.g., B. *Kiddushin* 45b). One of his roles was to convey to those in Babylonia the practices of the Land of Israel, and he was apparently invited by the Exilarch to lecture on this topic (B. *Ketubot* 65b; B. *Kiddushin* 31a; B. *Shabbat* 157b). So here we have two powerful, hot-tempered individuals who each have precedent for their practices and who are each determined to prevail. In such a case, Ulla's probably superior knowledge overcomes Yalta's social position . . . but just barely.

Women Who Insult Sages

While some, in fact, perhaps, many women, may have respected the sages and their authority, some of them did not and had to suffer the consequences. These women show that where there is no respect for learning and no self-restraint in expressing insult, there is no power. Before we examine the next passage, it will aid us to know that disrespectful behavior or flagrant breaches of discipline could result in different levels of isolation from the Jewish community. The most severe was *cherem*: excommunication from the Jewish people as a whole. In this state, a person is no longer considered a member of the community. Others are forbidden to stand within four cubits of this person or have commercial transactions with him or her. A less severe form of censure is *niddui*: ostracism or isolation. Persons in this state may not wear leather shoes or cut their hair and must keep four cubits from other Jews, although one may conduct business transactions with them. Between these two states is *sham'tta*. This ban is applied to a person who has been condemned to ostracism (*niddui*) and has still not mended his or her ways. The least-stringent form of isolation is *n'zifah*, "reproof," which involves isolation for one day. With this as background, we can understand the following text:

A certain woman was sitting sprawled on the footway fanning the husks out of her barley groats, and when a Collegiate was walking past her she did not make way for him. He said, "How impudent is this woman!" She came before Rav Nachman [who would decide if she should be excommunicated]. Said he to her, Did you hear him utter *sham'tta*? She said to him, "No." Said he to her, Go and submit yourself to the [disability of a] "reproof" (*n'zifah*) for one day. (B. *Mo'ed Katan* 16b)

This passage comes amidst many examples of sages unintentionally insulting each other and then laying on *themselves* the disability of "reproof." Our story differs from these others in some interesting ways. First of all, the offended party is the one who seems to be complaining, whereas in the other passages that surround this one, the offender himself realizes what he has done. What is really interesting, though, is that the insulter's gender makes no difference: it could have been a man or a woman. Therefore, it makes it somewhat more plausible that this case took place since we would not imagine the sages would make up a case with a woman in it when, if they were fabricating a case to teach legal theory, they would probably more readily choose a man as an exemplar.

And where is the power in this situation? There seems to be scant virtue exhibited in this interchange. The student seems to be a little too zealous for his own honor and the woman may simply have been busy and preoccupied with her work. Rav Nachman refuses to excommunicate her and gives her only the mildest form of censure, *n'zifah*, which lasts for one day. It is interesting that while Rabbi's maid could condemn someone to the much stricter *sham'tta* (B. *Mo'ed Katan* 17a) and have her sentence heeded, this student had to appeal to the authority of Rav Nachman to have even a lesser punishment enforced. Truly, the power is where the virtue resides.

In the last case we will examine, a woman shows great disrespect, both for the authority of the court and for a great sage. She is punished by earthly and heavenly authority. Again, we note with interest that the subject of this story could easily have been a man or a woman and so it seems somewhat more credible that a woman actually did the things recounted in this story.

A certain woman of Nehardea came before Rav Judah for a lawsuit and was declared guilty by the court. She said to him, "Would your teacher Samuel have judged thus?" He said to her, "Do you know him then?" She said to him, "Yes. He is short and big stomached, black and large teethed." He said to her, "You have come to insult him! Let that woman be under the ban (*sham'tta*)!" She burst and died. (B. *Nedarim* 50b)

A contemporary of Rav Nachman and Ulla, Rav Judah was one of the wisest and most spiritually powerful sages of his day. He founded the academy in Pumbedita, Babylonia, and was a disciple of the sage Samuel. He was renowned for his learning and his piety. The woman in this case seems to be his exact opposite: she lacks respect for the decisions of the court and for the teachers who formulated its rules. In this case, Rav Judah has virtue, and therefore power, on his side and it would appear that the heavenly court backs him up. He places her under a relatively strict ban, the *sham'tta*, after which she is reported to have died suddenly.

We are left with many questions about this woman. What was the case she brought before Rav Judah? Did she bring it before Samuel as well, as some commentators suggest, and was she hoping for a more lenient ruling from his student? What is the exact meaning of her insult? Is it a metaphorical referral to his specific judgment against her, or against his character, or is this perhaps an accurate description of his appearance? Did she really burst and die? If so, why? Was this woman, perhaps, simply one of those people who likes to have things her own way and didn't care about rules, roles, or respect? If so, we can then understand Rav Judah's reaction: he is not willing to be used by this woman for her own ends and his decree of a ban is confirmed by an even more severe heavenly decree. These questions obviously cannot be answered in an authoritative way, but one thing is clear, in this case as in all our others: virtue is power in the sages' system and has precious little to do with gender. Whoever acts out of virtue, whether in the private sphere of the family or the public spheres of the Temple, the courts, and the streets, is the one who is portrayed as powerful in our sources.

Today, there is no denying that money does bring power to those who have it. However, learning, goodness, putting in volunteer time, and philanthropy also convey power. At synagogue board meetings, those with money may speak, but they can always be "topped" by someone quoting a Jewish text in an authentic way. It reminds me of Temple David in Pittsburgh, the synagogue of my youth, which has a large wall dedicated to donors to the synagogue. The wall is divided in half. On one half are listed those who gave gifts of money. On the other half are those who gave the gift of their time. This is but one graphic demonstration of the sages' maxim: virtue, not money alone, is the source of power.

6

The Truth Will Out: Women's Testimony

Truth Telling and Rule Following

One of the things that bothers Americans most about our legal system, good as it is, are "legal technicalities" and rules that keep the whole truth from coming out in court for procedural reasons. The layperson, as opposed to lawyers, sees these rules as inherently unfair. We feel that a court is a place for truth telling more than rule following. Yet we also recognize that the law has to be administered according to some standard set of rules or a person found guilty in one court would be found innocent in another and that, too, would not be right.

The sages also experienced this tension. On the one hand, as we shall see, in capital cases, they had a vested interest in qualifying as few witnesses as possible since they were extremely reluctant to administer the death penalty. Thus, they excluded women from giving testimony. On the other hand, they were deeply committed to ferreting out the truth in court and recognized that women could provide that truth through their testimony. So there is inherent tension in the sages' system about allowing women to testify in court. How is it resolved? In general, the truth will out and women's testimony is considered valid. First, we will examine the texts that set up this tension and then we will examine the way women really functioned in court, according to our sources.

Other Exclusions

It may help us put the sages' exclusion of women from giving testimony into perspective if we first examine another passage that excludes whole classes of persons from giving testimony. The case under discussion in this mishnah is the "stubborn and rebellious son." The rules for dealing with such a child are outlined in the Torah.

> If a man have a stubborn and rebellious son, that will not hearken to the voice of his father or the voice of his mother, and though they chasten him, will not hearken unto them; then shall his father and his mother lay hold on him and bring him out unto the gate of his place; and they shall say unto the elders of his city: This our son is stubborn and rebellious, he does not hearken to our voice; he is a glutton and a drunkard. And all the men of his city shall stone him with stones, that he die; so shall you put away evil from the midst of you; and all Israel shall hear, and fear. (Deuteronomy 21:18–21)

This seemed a rather harsh punishment to the sages and so they tried, through interpretation of this passage from the Torah, to allow as few persons as possible to bring such charges against a child.

> If his father wanted [to bring him to the court for judgment], but his mother did not want to do so, [or] if his father did not want [to bring him to the court for judgment], but his mother did want to do so, he does not become a rebellious and disobedient son unless both of them want [to bring him to the court for judgment]. Rabbi Judah says, If his mother did not [look] like his father, he does not become a rebellious and disobedient son. If either of them had a maimed hand, or was lame, or was mute, or blind or deaf, he does not become a rebellious and disobedient son, as it is said, "then shall his father and his mother lay hold on him," and not those with a maimed hand [can lay hold on him]; "and bring him out," and not the lame [are able to bring him out]; "and they shall say," and not the mute [can so say]; "This is our son," and not such as are blind [are able to say thus, pointing to him]; "he does not hearken to our voice," and not the deaf [are able to hear]. (M. *Sanhedrin* 8:4)

In such cases, all sorts of people are disqualified from giving testimony against another person because the sages wanted to limit the number of such charges brought. In general, there is no reason, for example, that a person with a disability of hand or foot could not offer valid testimony. However, in this case, the sages were so opposed to the severity of the punishment that they limited who could testify by any means possible.

The Exclusion of Women

The restrictions against women's testimony are similarly enforced because some value within the sages' system is deemed more important than the inclusion of women in the process of giving testimony. The following verses from Numbers and Deuteronomy form the basis for the exclusion:

> And Moses went out and told the people the words of the Lord; and he gathered seventy men of the elders of the people and set them round about the Tent. And the Lord came down in the cloud and spoke unto him, and took of the spirit that was upon him, and put it upon the seventy elders; and it came to pass, that when the spirit rested upon them, they prophesied but they did so no more. But there remained in the camp *two men* (*shnei ha'anashim*) in the camp; the name of the one was Eldad and the name of the other Medad, and the spirit rested upon them, and they were of them that were recorded but had not gone out unto the Tent; and they prophesied in the camp. (Numbers 11:24–26)

> One witness shall not rise up against a man for any iniquity or for any sin, in any sin that he sins; at the mouth of two witnesses or at the mouth of three witnesses, shall a matter be established. If an unrighteous witness rise up against any man to bear perverted witness against him, then *both the men* (*shnei ha'anashim*) between whom the controversy is shall stand before the Lord, before the priests and the judges that shall be in those days. (Deuteronomy 19:15–17)

The following interpretation of these two verses excludes women from eligibility to act as witnesses:

> "The two men (Deuteronomy 19:17)": this can only mean two men . . . one might think therefore that a woman is qualified to act as a witness; [however, Scripture] says

"two" here (Deuteronomy 19:17) and "two" elsewhere (Numbers 11:26): just as "two" there refers to men and not to women, so "two" here refers to men and not to women. (*Sifre Deuteronomy* 190, parallel Y. *Yoma* 6:1, 43b–c)

The sages here are making use of a technique called the *gezeirah shavah*. This technique takes the way words are used in one place and assumes they mean the same thing in another place. They are applying this technique to the phrase *shnei ha'anashim*, "the two men" or "both the men." This phrase could also mean simply "two people" of either gender; however, the sages rule that it refers only to men. How? Just as, in the passage from Numbers, the phrase refers specifically to two *men*, Eldad and Medad, they assume that everywhere, for example, in the passage regarding witnessing in Deuteronomy, it must refer to two men and that therefore women are not qualified to serve as witnesses. This is the basis for excluding women from testifying in court. Nowhere does it explicitly state in the Torah, "Women may not testify in court." In other words, this exclusion comes from the sages and even they seem to have to search to find a basis for it in the Torah.

A Woman Testifies

So, in theory, women are excluded from giving testimony. However, when we examine accounts of women in court, the great value the sages placed on the truth seems to outweigh the gender of the person giving testimony and women are allowed to offer testimony. For example, we have a record in the *Mishnah* of a single, non-Jewish woman's testimony being accepted in the case of an *agunah*, a woman whose husband has disappeared without proper witnesses to his death, thus making it impossible for his widow to remarry. (Ordinarily, only two free Jewish males who had reached their majority, thirteen years old, could offer acceptable testimony.)

> It once happened that certain Levites went to Zoar, the City of Date Palms, and one of them became ill on the way and they brought him to an inn, and on their return they said to the woman innkeeper, "Where is our companon?" She said to them, "He died and I buried him," and they permitted his wife to be wed again. They answered him [Rabbi Akiba], "And should not a woman of priestly lineage be considered as [trustworthy as] a gentile mistress of an inn?" He said to them, "She will be deemed trustworthy [when she gives such evidence] as the woman innkeeper!" The woman innkeeper had brought out to them his staff and his bag and a Scroll of the Law he had with him. (M. *Yevamot* 16:7)

Here the *Mishnah* preserves a story in which a non-Jewish woman's testimony is accepted. Of course, her credibility is augmented by considerable material evidence. However, as related, this story allows such a person to give testimony in such a case. When the sages have a reason for relaxing the rules of testimony, they do so quite liberally. The problem of the *agunah* was, and is, one of the thorniest in Jewish law. The sages had a great vested interest in ameliorating such situations by any means at their disposal. One of those means was through liberalizing who could testify to a man's death, as we see here.

We should note, as well, that this is the very last passage in this entire tractate, a tractate that is quite theoretical in most of its considerations. The tractate ends with the most nontheoretical of stories, perhaps as a literary device, bringing the learner back to real-world considerations of death and loneliness that were the fate of the *agunah*.

The Daughters of a Sage Testify

What happens when truth and mercy are in conflict? This was a thorny issue that the daughters of a sage faced. Samuel's daughters were taken captive and used their knowledge of the following law to their advantage.

> The woman who says, "I was a married woman and I was divorced," is believed since the mouth that forbids is the mouth that permits. And if there are witnesses that she was married and she says, "I was divorced," she is not believed. She who says, "I was taken captive and I am clean," is believed, for the mouth that forbids is the mouth that permits. And if there are witnesses that she was made captive and she says, "I am clean," she is not believed. (M. *Ketubot* 2:5)

This mishnah is based on the principle that a woman would not voluntarily say something that could be detrimental to herself unless she was completely honest. Therefore, a woman wishing to marry might be better off saying, "I was never married" rather than, "I was married and divorced." However, if there were witnesses who could testify that she had been married, her assertion that she was divorced is not believed, since she had no choice but to confess that she had once been married. Likewise with the woman who was taken prisoner: if she confesses that she was taken prisoner but has not been raped, she is believed. However, if there are those who witnessed her in captivity, then her assertion that she had not been defiled is not believed since she has no choice but to make it. In this text from the *Yerushalmi*, Samuel's daughters manipulate the way they give testimony in a way that brings out what they claim is the truth but subverts the system of testimony.

> The daughters of Samuel were taken captive. . . . When they came up here, the captors came along with them. The case came before Rabbi Chaninah. [The women] kept the captors outside the courtroom. They said to [Rabbi Chaninah], "We were taken captive but we have remained clean." He then permitted them [to marry as undefiled women] . . . [Rabbi Chaninah] said, "You may be sure that these are the daughters of a sage [who knew enough to keep the captors outside the court, so that their testimony would fall within the frame of M. *Ketubot* 2:5]." (Y. *Ketubot* 2:6, 26c)

Since Samuel's daughters kept their captors outside the courtroom, and therefore there were no "available" witnesses, they could testify that they had been captured and yet were undefiled, according to the law. Here we see women, expert in the law, using their expertise to their advantage. They are able to offer testimony. However, we have an indication in the subsequent commentary on this episode that the sages disapproved of what they did, for they both died soon thereafter and the question is raised as to whether this was because they kept the full truth from coming out in court. This suggestion is rejected, but it shows that there was ambivalence about their actions. The sages' ambivalence is probably not related to the issue of gender here, though we cannot say this conclusively.

A Woman Testifies to Become Divorced

Of course, both men and women could come into court seeking to offer lies as testimony and the sages' goal, regardless of the gender of the person before them, was to determine the truth. For example, in the following case, a woman is presumed to be giving testimony in order to force her husband to give her a divorce. This motivation of hers casts doubt on her testimony.

> Soldiers came into a city, and a woman came and said, "Soldiers embraced me and had sexual relations with me." And [Chananiah nonetheless] permitted her to eat *terumah*. (Y. *Nedarim* 11:13, 42d)

This case is brought as a comment on M. *Nedarim* 11:12, the last mishnah in the entire tractate, which describes three sorts of women who, in earlier days, had immediately been granted divorces but who now are delayed in this process by various measures. One of these sorts of women is the one who says, "I am unclean for you [i.e., I have been unfaithful to you]." In earlier times, she was simply believed and granted a divorce, but now she must bring proof that she was unfaithful. In other words, apparently this technique was used by women who wanted to force their husbands to grant them divorces. They knew that all they had to say was, "I have been unfaithful," and the divorce would be theirs. To obviate this easy road to divorce, they were therefore required to provide proof of their unfaithfulness.

Apparently the woman who came to R. Chananiah wanted to divorce her husband. She had fabricated this story about the soldiers raping her in order to free herself from her husband, a priest. Since he was a priest and was allowed to eat *terumah*, that portion of every farmer's crop given to a priest and his family, she, as his wife, could also eat *terumah* as long as she ate it in a state of ritual purity. If R. Chananiah had believed that she had actually been raped, he would not have permitted her to eat *terumah*, since rape would render her unfit to be his wife. And since she could not be his wife, she could not receive *terumah* anymore. But since R. Chananiah did not believe any part of her tale, suspecting that she had concocted it in order to be free of her husband, he kept her in her marriage, symbolized by her continuing ability to eat *terumah*. R. Chananiah was devoted to the truth, which he did not feel was revealed by this woman's testimony.

This is a frequent problem in the law. R. Chananiah seems to know something that is not preserved in our records. Perhaps her husband was a well-known lout, which caused suspicion that she wanted to be free of him. Or perhaps she had even stated that she wanted him to divorce her. Whether the laws of Jewish divorce are fair and whether she should have been able to obtain a divorce without all this subterfuge are not what interest us here. For our purposes, what is interesting is that she is allowed to offer testimony despite her gender but that, clearly, truth is the goal, and when her testimony does not serve to further that goal, it is disregarded.

A Woman and Her Witnesses

Sometimes a woman was not believed in court, not because she was too expert in the law and could manipulate it, or because the sages thought she was lying, but because those she brought to corroborate her story were not seen as reliable witnesses themselves.

The following case, which is an example of this latter phenomenon, is brought up in a passage exploring the complicated laws regarding *eidim zomemim*, "conspiring witnesses." These laws are based on the following passage from the Torah:

> One witness shall not rise up against a man for any iniquity or for any sin, in any sin that he sins; at the mouth of two witnesses, or at the mouth of three witnesses, shall a matter be established. If an unrighteous witness rise up against any man to bear perverted witness against him then both the men, between whom the controversy is, shall stand before the Lord, before the priests and the judges that shall be in those days. And the judges shall inquire diligently; and behold, if the witness be a false witness, and has testified falsely against his brother; then shall you do to him as he planned to do unto his brother; so shall you put evil from your midst. (Deuteronomy 19:15–19)

This passage establishes several important principles regarding Jewish judicial proceedings. First, a single witness may not testify. Two witnesses must testify to an event. Second, if the witnesses have conspired to fabricate testimony against a person and are subsequently impeached as false witnesses, the punishment they sought to have inflicted on the accused is inflicted on them instead (with many limitations). The problem of multiple *eidim zomemim* is dealt with in this mishnah:

> [If] further [sets of witnesses] came, and they were proved false witnesses, even up to a hundred [sets], they are all put to death [in capital cases]. Rabbi Judah says, "This is a conspiracy and only the first set [of false witnesses] is executed." (M. *Makkot* 1:5)

What is our main problem here? The sages were committed to two competing principles in capital cases: they wanted to minimize loss of life and they wanted to be sure truth and justice were served. The majority of sages, as represented in this mishnah, feel that justice and truth outweigh loss of life. Rabbi Judah, on the other hand, seems more committed to minimizing loss of life. His view is a minority opinion and is not accepted. We might keep in mind that at the time the *Mishnah* was compiled (200 C.E.) Jewish courts had long since been stripped of the ability to administer capital punishment, and so these rulings were completely theoretical. However, the problem of multiple lying witnesses in a *non-capital-punishment* case remained and it is in this connection that the following case is brought:

> There was a certain woman who brought [her] witnesses and they were discredited; she brought [others], and they [too] were discredited; she went and brought further witnesses who were not discredited. Said Reish Lakish: This woman is suspect. Said Rabbi Eleazar to him: "Assuming she is suspect, are all Israel to be held as suspects?" (B. *Makkot* 5b)

Here we have a woman who brings two sets of witnesses who are discredited. (This is different from conspiring witnesses, *eidim zomemim*, but is thematically related.) Perhaps there were inconsistencies in their testimony that were brought out during questioning. In any case, the third set of witnesses was not discredited by questioning, yet Reish Lakish wanted to reject their testimony since he felt that this woman was disreputable and seemed liable to bringing false witnesses. Rabbi Eleazar retorts that we cannot discredit witnesses simply because they are testifying on behalf of a disreputable person. (Being considered a valid witness was something of a stamp of approval on a person's character and, likewise, being discredited from giving testimony spoke against a person. For example, those engaged in sharp business dealings were never eligible to give testimony [M. *Sanhedrin* 3:3]. Thus, denying someone's ability to testify might be perceived or experienced as doing them harm.)

In the end, the concern for the truth, and the possibility that these witnesses' testimony could be true outweighed the suspicions generated by the first two sets of disqualified witnesses. We note that this case history would have worked as well with a man as the protagonist as with a woman, and therefore it seems relatively more likely that the case actually took place as reported. From across the centuries, we can feel empathy for this woman. To stand accused, and to stand and give testimony in court, are frightening experiences. No matter how much one tries to avoid it, one brings one's social class and education into the courtroom experience. Was this woman simply poor or uneducated, unfamiliar with the rules of the court? Or was she truly conniving? We cannot know, of course, but we can easily imagine her desperation and fear as she sought and brought forward her three sets of witnesses and her relief when their testimony was finally admitted.

In all these cases, a woman's right to enter the court and plead for justice is never questioned. The courts were open to all and their dual goals were to reveal the truth and to dispense justice balanced with mercy. If preventing a woman from giving testimony or pleading her case were to impair the search for the truth, a way was found around this exclusion. And, it appears from our stories of women in court, some women did in fact come forward to seek justice from the sages.

Today, in secular society, with women serving as judges and advocates, women's equality in the courtroom is improving. In Jewish life, women are still not able to serve as witnesses in many instances. Hopefully, the desire to include women in the processes of Jewish life will soon override all other competing values that now lead to women's exclusion from giving testimony.

7

Diffidence and Distance: The Sages and Childbirth, Nursing, and Motherhood

Women's "*Gemara*"

Gather any group of women who have had children and they will be able to tell you ritualized stories of each of their children's births and childhoods. They can recount how long labor lasted, whether they had anesthetic, whether they nursed or bottle fed, how they dealt with chicken pox, and they can discuss whether infancy or adolescence is a more difficult phase of life. These topics give women something in common no matter how unbridgeable the gulfs between them are in the other spheres of their lives. This is probably somewhat like men who can discuss sports with other men who are otherwise perfect strangers.

These women's stories, which would undoubtedly be included in a *Gemara* written by women, are almost completely lacking in our sources. This is not completely surprising. There are some experiences that men simply cannot fully participate in, no matter how interested or empathetic they may be. No matter how supportive a man may be as a labor coach, childbirth does not hurt him. No matter how nurturing he may be, he cannot nurse an infant.

How did the sages respond to these facts of human existence? The sages were, after all, an entirely male group. How did they react to the spheres of human experience that were exclusively female domains? One way the sages responded to the experiences that epitomize a woman's (to them) "otherness" was to idealize the relationships in this separate sphere. Another way they responded was by attempting to legislate what happened during the processes of childbirth and nursing. However, in practice, when we look at the case histories preserved for us in rabbinic literature, we find that the sages did recognize that women were expert in these areas, shared their authority with women regarding these matters, and even allowed women control over these domains.

This is not merely an ancient phenomenon. Susan Starr Sered, in her book *Women as Ritual Experts*, outlines the ways that women function as ritual experts today in domains separate from religion as it is defined by men.[1] This suggests, although it will have to be proven by a rigorous scholarly review of our sources, that there may always have been domains in Jewish life that women controlled and that men recognized as being under women's control. We can begin that inquiry by examining the idealized way the sages framed motherhood and then by looking at how they allowed women great control over the fundamental processes of motherhood: pregnancy and nursing.

The Idealization of Motherhood:
High Priests and Their Mothers

If we were to picture the idealized form of maternal gratification today, we might imagine it resides in the president's mother, or the mother of some other high-achieving child. The sages also imagined maternal gratification in this way. In their case, the ideal children who would give ultimate gratification to a mother were high priests and sages who took the precept of honoring their mothers to new heights. (In fact, we seem to see a shift from our earlier to our later sources away from priests and toward sages as "ultimate children." This is natural since, after the Temple's destruction in 70 c.e., the priesthood became less of a focal point for social organization in the Jewish world and the sages gradually gained more influence.) For example, one mother, who saw two of her sons officiate as high priests on the same day, seems to have been the ultimate example of maternal *nachus* (gratification).

> It is told of Simeon ben Qimchit that he went forth to speak with the king in the evening and spit spurted out of his [the king's] mouth and fell on his [Simeon ben Qimchit's] clothes. His brother went in and served in his stead as high priest. The mother of these [men] witnessed two [officiating] high priests [who were her sons] on the same day. (T. *Kippurim* 3:20)

A little background may make this passage more comprehensible. The high priest had to officiate in a state of absolute purity at all times; all the more so on Yom Kippur. The king may not have been in a state of ritual purity and when his spit made contact with the priest, the priest was thereby disqualified from officiating at the cult for that day. Apparently, Simeon ben Qimchit (high priest in 17–18 c.e.) began the day (which begins at sundown) as the officiating high priest but had to step down from officiating the next day since this incident happened in the evening. Therefore, his brother stepped in and took his place. What is interesting is that this is characterized as the height of maternal, but not paternal, or spousal, satisfaction, perhaps because a woman could not hope to officiate in this role herself. Today, thankfully, women don't have to live out the vast majority of their ambitions through their children, male or female.

Mothers were apparently quite invested in their sons' positions as high priests. For example, a mother (again, apparently not a wife) could play a role in achieving the ultimate gratification of having a son officiate as a high priest on Yom Kippur by providing her son with a lavish outfit for the occasion.

> "If he wanted to add, he may add out of his own pocket (M. *Yoma* 3:7)." It is told that Ishmael b. Piabi's mother made him a tunic worth a hundred *manehs*. And he would stand and make offerings on the altar [while wearing it].
>
> R. Eleazar ben Harsom's mother made for him a tunic for twenty thousand, and he would stand and make offerings on the altar [while wearing it]. But his brethren, the priests, called him down [from the altar], because [it was so sheer that] he appeared naked [while wearing it]. (T. *Kippurim* 1:21–22)

According to the *Mishnah* (M. *Yoma* 3:7), the garb for high priests officiating on Yom Kippur was paid for from public funds donated to the Temple. However, if an individual high priest wished to make his outfit more lavish and spend his own money to make it so, he was entitled to do so. Apparently, two high priests' mothers made quite elaborate outfits for their sons to officiate in. To understand the value of these tunics, we can compare them with those described in this mishnah that were worth between twelve and thirty *manehs*. There seems to be a bit of criticism of R. Eleazar ben Harsom's tunic. Apparently it was so finely made that it was transparent. Perhaps part of the pageantry of Yom Kippur was the spectacle of the priests' robes, not unlike the fashion show that the High Holidays (unfortunately) can be today. Striking the balance between wearing finery appropriate to the solemnity of the occasion, which helps one pray, and focusing too much on one's clothes, was apparently as difficult then as it is now.

Sons Honoring Mothers and Vice Versa

Idealized gratification and devotion are not a one-way street in our sources. Sons could go to great lengths to honor their mothers as well as vice versa. (These idealized relationships tend to be framed in terms of mother–son bonds rather than those between mother and daughter.)

> Rabbi Tarfon's mother went down for a walk in her courtyard on the Sabbath. [Her slipper came off, and she would not retie it, because that would be a violation of Sabbath laws.] Rabbi Tarfon, [not wanting his mother's feet to become sore,] went and placed his two hands under her feet, so that she could walk upon them all the way to her couch.
>
> One time, [Rabbi Tarfon] became ill, and the sages came in to visit him. [His mother] said to them, "Pray for Tarfon my son, for he treats me with far too much re-

spect!" They said to her, "What did he do for you?" She
told them [the foregoing] story. They said to her, "Even
if he were to do so thousands of thousands [of times],
still he would not attain even half [the measure] that the
Torah commands [for honor of one's mother]!"

Rabbi Ishmael's mother came and complained against
[her son] before our rabbis. She said to them, "Rebuke
Ishmael my son, for he does not treat me with respect!"
At that moment our rabbis' faces flushed [with embar-
rassment]. They said, "Is it possible that Rabbi Ishmael
would not treat his parents with respect?" [So] they said
to her, "What did he do to you?" She said, "When he left
the [scholars'] meeting place I wanted to wash his feet
and drink the water, but he wouldn't let me, [thereby
showing me disrespect]!" They said to [Rabbi Ishmael],
"Since this is her wish, this is [what you must do as a
mode of] honoring her." (Y. *Pe'ah* 1:1, 15c // Y. *Kiddushin*
1:7, 61b // B. *Kiddushin* 31b)

These stories are part of a much longer passage about
the almost infinite merit of honoring one's parents. Rabbi
Tarfon's mother feels that her son's attentions are excessive, but the sages assure her that he is only giving her
the honor due her. Rabbi Ishmael's mother wants to show
him what he considers excessive, and perhaps idiosyncratic, respect. Rabbi Ishmael declines to grant his mother's
wish, but the sages rule that he must accede to her de-
mands. These are clearly idealized and exaggerated forms
of honor on both Rabbi Tarfon's and Rabbi Ishmael's
mothers' parts.

It may have been natural that such legends grew up
around the characters of Rabbi Tarfon and Rabbi Ishmael.
Rabbi Tarfon, a priest, was one of the greatest sages in
the generation after the Temple's destruction in 70 c.e.
He was a contemporary of Rabbi Akiba and was esteemed

as one of the greatest scholars of his day. In addition, many legends about his righteousness can be found in rabbinic literature, including one that claims he betrothed three hundred girls in a year of famine so that they, as women betrothed to a priest, could eat *terumah* (T. *Ketubot* 5:1) and therefore would not starve. Rabbi Ishmael, like Rabbi Tarfon, was a priest and sage in the first half of the second century c.e. who witnessed the Temple's destruction as a boy. Also like Rabbi Tarfon, he is portrayed as being quite kind to women, helping them beautify themselves in order to facilitate their getting married (e.g., Y. *Nedarim* 9:9 reports that he provided a woman with a prosthetic eye and tooth to make her more attractive). In addition, he was one of the greatest scholars of his day, developing a system of textual interpretation that differed from Rabbi Akiba's. So both Rabbi Tarfon and Rabbi Ishmael embodied a later ideal of maternal gratification: men who were righteous and learned, priests and sages, honoring women and especially honoring their mothers.

Actually, in this case, the Jewish ideal relationship between mothers and children does not seem to have changed dramatically over the centuries, except that now, perhaps, the righteous rabbi-child can also be a daughter. Parenting has always been a difficult job to do in a way that merits honor. Would that parents would devote themselves to this task . . . and would that children would respond with such honor for their parents!

The Sages in the Waiting Room: Childbirth, Nursing, and Women's Domain

Not so very long ago it was standard practice for men to sit, waiting anxiously in some separate room while their wives gave birth to their children in another room. They might have had some indirect input into the proceedings but basically, they were kept out of this process. This image is an apt one when describing the process of childbirth in the sages' day, as well. The sages nominally legislated the processes of childbirth, particularly when those processes intersected with areas of Jewish law that the sages did adjudicate with authority, such as Sabbath restrictions. However, when we examine our case histories we see that the sages allowed women to regulate the processes of childbirth and infant care to a remarkably great extent.

For example, even when a question is addressed to a sage on a matter about which he does have authority to give an answer, such as permissible violations of Sabbath restrictions during childbirth, the sage defers to women's customs. Of course, the sages had come up with a theoretical approach to the problem of childbirth on the Sabbath.

They may deliver a woman on *Shabbat*, and they summon a midwife for her from anyplace, and profane the *Shabbat* on her account, and tie up the navel. Rabbi Yose says, "They even cut it." (M. *Shabbat* 18:3)

Rabbi Yose's opinion is an individual opinion and, therefore, we would think it is not accepted as law. In general, only the opinions of the anonymous majority are accepted as law and individual opinions, though important, do not become law. His opinion here is that the umbilical cord may be cut, an additional profanation of the *Shabbat* that the majority apparently feels need not be performed, the tying off of the cord being enough. We find in the following case, however, that Rabbi Yose's opinion is the one used in practice.

A servant girl of Bar Qappara went and brought forth a child on the Sabbath. A woman came and asked Rabbi [whether they might tie and cut the umbilical cord]. He said to her, "Go and ask the midwife." She said to him, "There is no midwife [here]." He said to her, "Go and follow your usual practice." She said to him, "There is no established practice." He said to her, "Go and cut [the umbilical cord], in line with the view of Rabbi Yose." (M. *Shabbat* 18:3) (Y. *Shabbat* 18:3)

In this case, practice actually followed Rabbi Yose's view, but what is really interesting is that Rabbi would rather not offer an opinion and would prefer to leave it up to the midwife. However, when cornered, he offers a lenient ruling based on an individual's opinion.

This whole scenario makes us wonder how many of these decisions were left up to midwives and the women they aided. Rabbi is willing to let a midwife, or even any woman attending the birth, decide this issue. Was there a whole set of birth lore and standard rules of practice related to birth of which the sages were ignorant? This passage seems to suggest that such could have been the case. Rabbi certainly echoes males' sense of superfluousness during labor and delivery, even if they serve as labor coaches. Labor is an experience men cannot share (nor do they probably wish to do so!).

Abaye's Nurse and Her Teachings

Another text that suggests women may have developed and transmitted a corpus of knowledge about birthing and infant care is a long string of teachings about newborn care recorded in the name of Abaye's nurse. Abaye (280–338 C.E.) was a great Babylonian scholar who was orphaned as an infant (B. *Kiddushin* 31b) and was raised by a foster mother, known as "nurse." Abaye quotes her extensively and, from this material, we get a picture of a woman who was extremely knowledgeable in the medical lore of her day. We know almost nothing else about her and we do not know her name. However, her teachings have survived for us to study. Abaye deserves much of the credit for this. He obviously considered her a knowledgeable authority and quotes the information in her name rather than his own.

While many of Abaye's nurse's medical teachings would not be considered valid today, some of her teachings about newborn diagnosis and resuscitation are still fairly accurate.

Abaye also said: Mother told me, An infant whose anus is not visible should be rubbed with oil and stood in the sun, and where it shows transparent it should be torn crosswise with a barley grain, but not with a metal instrument, because that causes inflammation.

Abaye also said: Mother told me, If an infant cannot suck, his lips are cold. What is the remedy? A vessel of burning coals should be brought and held near his nostrils, so as to heat it, then he will suck.

Abaye also said: Mother told me, If an infant does not breathe he should be fanned with a fan and he will breathe.

Abaye also said: Mother told me, If an infant cannot breathe easily, his mother's afterbirth should be brought and rubbed over him, [and] he will breathe easily.

Abaye also said: Mother told me, If an infant is too thin, his mother's afterbirth should be brought and rubbed over him from its narrow end to its wide end; if he is too fat [it should be rubbed] from the wide to the narrow end.

Abaye also said: Mother told me, If an infant is too red, so that the blood is not yet absorbed in him, we must wait until his blood is absorbed and then circumcise him. If he is green, so that he is deficient in blood, we must wait until he is full blooded and then circumcise him. (B. *Shabbat* 134a)

Although our methods of treating newborns have changed over the centuries, stimulating them and making sure they are warm, fed, and cared for are still primary goals of newborn care. What is truly interesting is that a woman is the recognized authority on these issues. Were women generally the experts about childbirth? Would these rules about newborn care have had more, or less, credibility had they been recited in a man's name? We may suspect that they are more credible when cited in a woman's name, else the text would simply cite the teachings in Abaye's name alone since it was he who reported them.

Pregnant Women and Fasting

Another example of the sages allowing women to decide some issues of pregnancy for themselves is found in the commentary to the following mishnah:

A pregnant woman who smelled [food and drink on Yom Kippur] they feed her until she recovers [her senses]. (M. *Yoma* 8:5)

Must a pregnant woman fast on Yom Kippur? The *Bavli* explains that a pregnant woman is fed gradually, and only just enough so that she recovers, although, if she absolutely must eat pork to satisfy herself, even on Yom Kippur, she may do so (B. *Yoma* 82a). The sages of the *Bavli* seem to recognize that they can contribute to this decision-making process only through suggestion rather than through legislation.

> There was a woman with child who had smelt [a dish].
> [People] came before Rabbi [questioning him what should be done]. He said to them: Go and whisper to her that it is the Day of Atonement. They whispered to her and she accepted the whispered suggestion, [whereupon] he [Rabbi] cited about her [the verse]: "Before I formed you in the belly I knew you" (Jeremiah 1:5). From her came forth Rabbi Jochanan.
>
> [Again] there was a woman with child who had smelt [a dish]. [People] came before Rabbi [questioning him what should be done]. He said to them: Go and whisper to her that it is the Day of Atonement. They whispered to her and she did not accept the whispered suggestion. He cited with regard to her, "The wicked are estranged from the womb" (Psalm 58:4). From her came forth Shabbatia, the hoarder of provisions [for speculation]. (B. *Yoma* 82b–83a)

Rabbi does not issue a ruling here. Rather, he offers suggestions and allows the woman to decide how to handle this difficulty in her pregnancy. We also see here an apparent ancient belief in the "nature over nurture" theory of personality: the child's future moral character is already formed in the womb. Sages, of course, were held in the highest esteem, and those who hoarded food for profit during famines were considered the lowest of the low. So each fetus was already exhibiting its nature through the cravings of its mother. The sages apparently felt that it was the fetus, not the mother, who developed the craving.

Nursing

In a different case, the sages recognize the uniqueness of the mother–infant bond as they develop into a nursing pair. It is important to remember that the only nutrition available to a newborn in this era was human milk so a child had to be nursed, either by its mother or by a wet nurse. The sages mandated that nursing should continue for two years and could continue for as long as five years if the child and mother so desired. However, some women did not want to nurse for even the minimum required two years if they were divorced or widowed, since this nursing relationship prevented them from remarrying. (Nursing women could not be remarried during this two-year nursing period lest they become pregnant by their new husbands, thereby decreasing their milk supply and putting their babies in danger.) In one case involving a divorcée reluctant to continue nursing her child, the sages show great sensitivity to the mother–child bond.

A [divorced woman] once came before Samuel [declaring her refusal to nurse her son]. He said to Rav Dimi bar Joseph, "Go and test her case [to see if the child recognizes his mother]." He went and placed her among a row of women and, taking hold of her child, carried him in front of them. When he came up to her [the child] looked at her face, but she turned her eye away from him. He said to her, "Lift up your eyes, come, take away your son." How does a blind child know [its mother]? Rav Ashi said: By the smell and the taste [of the milk]. (B. Ketubot 60a)

This case is brought in a discussion of when, exactly, a woman no longer has the option of using a wet nurse rather than nursing her infant herself. The sages feel that once the child has become accustomed to its mother, it would not accept a wet nurse and the woman is compelled to nurse her own child. In this case, a woman divorces her husband and wants Samuel to allow her to engage a wet nurse for the infant. Rav Dimi bar Joseph then conducts the experiment and the child responds to its mother. Therefore, she is compelled to nurse the baby. Once more, we find the sages willing to base their decisions on the individual women and children involved in a case rather than relying solely on theoretical rules. Incidentally, the findings of the sages in this regard are remarkably consistent with modern medicine's view of a newborn's perceptions. A newborn can recognize its mother's voice and odor quite quickly after birth.

Nursing is, in America, a private relationship; an extension of the physical bond of pregnancy in a less intense form. The mother and child need each other: the child requires nutrition and the woman needs the child to nurse if she is to maintain her health. Again, men may witness this process but cannot actively participate in it to a great extent. And deciding when to wean is also a woman's decision that she makes together with her baby.

In all these cases, we seem to have indications that pregnancy, childbirth, and nursing were areas in which the sages were willing to defer to the practice and authority of women. They could suggest appropriate actions to be taken, but from a distance. They seem to have recognized that the real authorities in these areas were women. The sages' combination of idealization and respect suggests that they felt a certain distance between themselves and women as mothers. They seem almost star struck in their romantic portrayals of maternal devotion and well nigh speechless in the face of women giving birth and nurturing young life. We will find similar ambivalence on their parts as we explore how they dealt with women's sexuality, menstruation, and fertility in our next chapter.

8

Judgment and Jealousy: The Sages, Sex, and Ritual Purity

I was recently going through my closet and discarding clothes that no longer fit me. However, there were some clothes that, no matter how outdated or ill fitting, I could not throw away. The dress I wore for my civil wedding ceremony held such good memories, and the suit I was wearing at the moment my father died held such painful ones, that I could not part with them. The sages held that the emotions and memories that adhere to physical objects are real. Ritual purity is their way of objectifying and regulating these feelings and forces as they relate to life and death.

Ritual Purity and Impurity: The Basics

In Judaism, perhaps more than in other systems of religious thought, life is holy and death is profane. So, for example, we find it a natural expression of Jewish values when God says in the Torah, "See, I have set before you this day life and good and death and evil" (Deuteronomy 30:15). Life is naturally paired with good and death with evil. This is not necessarily the case in other religions, but it is axiomatic in Jewish thought.

This basic premise is put into action in the world through the system of ritual purity and impurity. This system can be summed up with a simple equation: the closer an item is to death the more impure it will be. Thus, the most impure thing in Judaism is a corpse, the embodiment of death. Anything that is connected with death, or with the absence of life, is considered impure, and this impurity can be transferred to the objects that come in contact with an impure person or substance. So menstrual blood, and the menstruating woman, called a *niddah*, are considered ritually impure because menstruation means that fertilization has not taken place. Similarly, semen is considered impure as is the man who has emitted it. Impurity is called *tumah* and purity is called *taharah* in rabbinic literature. Over time, most of the rules regarding ritual purity and impurity ceased to be observed. However, the system continued to be a powerful way of dealing with the important psychological and spiritual feelings people have about life and death.

To help us understand the role rules about ritual purity, which were largely connected to the Temple, played in ancient Israelite society, we can compare them to the role hospitals and their rules about sterility play in our society today. These two institutions have striking similarities. Each is operated by personnel organized into a rather strict hierarchy. Just as in the Temple there were high priests, regular priests, and Levites who helped the priests in their tasks, so hospitals have departmental chiefs, physicians, nurses, technicians, and the like.

There were strict rules of purity that had to be adhered to in the Temple: the priests could only officiate in a state of ritual purity. Similarly, strict rules of purity adhere to hospitals. Just as there was a "Holy of Holies" in the Temple, to which access was extremely limited, so we have operating rooms in hospitals that are subject to the strictest rules of antisepsis, and have the least public access. Just as a priest's manner when offering a sacrifice was secondary to his correct offering of the animal, so a physician's bedside manner is not primary. We will tolerate the gruffest surgeon if he or she is sufficiently proficient technically. Finally, both are places conceived of as centers for healing. Just as we enter a hospital hoping to be transformed from illness to health, so did ancient Israelites come to the Temple hoping for transformation from a sinful state to a sanctified one, or from illness to health.

In this chapter, we will explore the issue of purity and impurity from two basic perspectives. First, we will look at it in its ritual and legal manifestations. Much of the case material regarding women in rabbinic literature explores legislation about ritual purity in action: the classification of specimens of blood brought to different authorities and the sort of ritual impurity, if any, these types of blood conveyed. These passages will reveal that the sages shared authority with women in this area, as they did regarding childbirth and nursing. Second, we will examine a lengthy passage that reveals the sages' underlying thoughts on the conundrum that was woman: a person who embodies both death (menstrual blood) and life (a fetus) on a recurring basis. In this passage, one sage seems to take on these characteristically female traits.

This story is quite difficult to understand, yet so many women are active in it, and it touches on our subject so deeply, that it could not be excluded. Nonetheless, those who find it too difficult (not to mention somewhat bizarre) may want to skip it and move on to the next chapter.

The Sages and Women: Sharing Authority over Ritual Purity

We tend to think of the sages as arbiters and authority figures who could decree, "Thus shall it be!" and thus it was. This is a romantic view of the sages. As many scholars have shown, the sages in the rabbinic era had to "sell" people on their view of Judaism much more than they could simply "tell" them what to do. Of course, if we think about our relationships with rabbis today, and extrapolate from them, we will see that it was unlikely that the sages would have uncontested authority. Even the most respected rabbis today share authority with those they lead and many rabbis must do quite a bit of "selling." And if they do too much "telling" they may find themselves looking for another job! Thus, it should not surprise us that we find recorded in our sources a wide range of power and authority ascribed to the sages in their role as authority figures regarding women and ritual purity. Just as, today, some people tend to accept their rabbi's authority to a greater extent than others do, there were women in the rabbinic era who apparently did consult the sages on these matters. And just as there are people today who negotiate with their rabbis or ignore what their rabbis tell them, there were women who shared authority with the sages or acted as sages themselves in arbitrating these matters. We will see examples of the entire gamut of attitudes in the passages that follow.

Intention and Ritual Impurity

A woman in a state of ritual impurity due to the fact that she was menstruating could, according to the Torah, convey impurity to persons, utensils, and clothes that she touched (Leviticus 19: 15–24). This ruling could have economic consequences, as we see in this passage.

> One woman was weaving a cloth in cleanness, and she came before R. Ishmael for inspection. She said to him, "Rabbi, I know that the cloth was not made unclean, but it was not in my heart to guard it [from impurity]." In the course of the questions R. Ishmael asked her, she said to him, "Rabbi, I know that a menstruating woman came and pulled the rope with me." Said R. Ishmael, "How great are the words of sages who would say, 'If one did not intend to guard it, it is unclean.'" (T. *Keilim Bava Batra* 1:2)

Contrary to popular belief, intentions *are* important in Judaism. We are accustomed to thinking, "It doesn't matter what I think; as long as I don't commit X [a sin] it's okay." While in general in Judaism this is true—that is, you will, for example, not be held liable by God for *wanting* to eat bacon but only for actually *eating* it—it is not true that intentions are unimportant. Indeed, intentions, what a person thinks about an object, are crucial in defining that object. If I look at a pinecone and see food and intend to eat it, then it is considered food, according to the sages. If I look at a pinecone and see an inedible plant form, then the pinecone is not considered food in

this instance in the sages' system. So intentions are criti-
cal when deciding how physical items in a given environ-
ment are categorized.

In this passage, the intentions of the woman have defi-
nite consequences. The woman did not intend to guard
the materials she was working on from impurity and therefore they did become impure. We can understand this by
thinking of a different example. Let us say that a lab technician draws a vial of blood from a person who has hepatitis. However, the technician, not knowing the blood contains this virus, does not wear gloves while drawing it and
does not take precautions about spilling it because she
is unaware that it contains the virus. Her supervisor, in
investigating the incident, would question this technician
about her procedures and what she has done with the
blood in determining if her handling of the blood put anyone at risk for contracting the virus. As a general rule, this
supervisor might mandate that any blood that has been
drawn should be treated as if it contained the hepatitis
virus.

The woman in our passage was weaving cloth in a state
of ritual purity but did not take precautions lest it come
in contact with any uncleanness from anyone else.
Did she cause the cloth to become impure? R. Ishmael
questions her and it turns out that she did let a menstruating woman, who is considered ritually impure, help her
make the cloth and therefore the cloth is unclean. The
point of the story from the sages' point of view is the
wisdom of the maxim "Consider everything that was not
guarded as unclean," or, to use our analogy again, "Consider every blood sample to have the hepatitis virus."
When we think about the actual women involved in this
case, we see that the sages' decisions could have real-life

consequences for women's relationships with each other, consequences with which the sages do not seem to concern themselves.

Ritual Purity and Jewish Diversity

The woman in our last passage goes to a sage as an authority on ritual purity. However, we must consider that many women did not concern themselves with what the sages thought. Indeed, many Jews, men and women, did not follow the sages' system at all. Jews have always been a heterogeneous group. Today, relatively few Jewish women follow the laws of *niddah* or go to the *mikveh* for any reason, even though these laws are still in force. Yet it should be noted that some women are starting to reclaim the *mikveh* as a mechanism that helps them ritualize transitions. For example, a ritual using the *mikveh* as a way to cope with the aftermath of rape has been developed. This may not be the exact way the sages thought about issues of ritual purity and the *mikveh*, but it is a logical outgrowth of their thinking. Any Jewish woman can use the *mikveh* at any time. She will most likely not be questioned about her motives for doing so. Therefore, women are free to use the *mikveh* in ways that are meaningful to them, whether it is to follow *halakhah* or to mark private turning points in their lives.

The rules of *niddah* may have been a point of solidarity within the Jewish people in ancient days. Before the destruction of the Temple, the Sadducees and Pharisees differed on the interpretation of the Torah and many Jewish practices. However, apparently there were some areas of agreement between the two groups. They evidently shared a system of evaluating a woman's state of ritual purity or impurity.

> It is told that a Sadducean chatted with a high priest, and spit spurted from his mouth and fell on the garments of the high priest, and the face of the high priest blanched. Then they came and asked his [the Saducee's] wife, and she said, "My lord priest: Even though we are Sadducean women, they [we] all bring their inquiries to a sage."
>
> Said R. Yose, "We are more expert in the Sadducean women than anyone. For they all bring their questions to a sage, except for one who was among them, and she died." (T. Niddah 5:3)

A high priest, like any priest, had to maintain himself in a state of ritual purity in order to officiate at the Temple cult and reap some of the benefits of the priesthood. For example, if a priest was in an impure state he could not eat terumah, that part of every crop that was given to the priests and their families for their personal consumption. So when this Sadducee inadvertently spat on this high priest's garments, the priest worried that he had become ritually impure. However, the Sadducee's wife reassured the priest that she, and the other women of her group, took their questions of ritual purity to duly recognized authorities, meaning sages. We suspect that the final story about the one Sadducean woman who failed to consult a sage about these matters and who died is a bit of hyperbole and/or reinterpretation after the fact of her demise.

Perhaps we can understand this woman by using the following analogy. Most people today consult with physicians. However, some do not do so because they are either too busy, hostile to doctors, are afraid of treatment, or simply do not think that doctors have anything to offer them. Those who do consult doctors might consider the case of someone who did not and who then died as an example of how dangerous it is *not* to consult with doctors.

These two cases seem designed to show the sages' uncontested authority to decide questions of ritual purity. For that reason we must regard them skeptically. In addition, the protagonist in these stories has to be a woman. Therefore, we should be quite cautious before jumping to conclusions about how frequently women actually consulted with the sages about these matters based on these passages.

Yalta Shares Authority with Sages

Just as some women and men seem to be cowed by their relationships with sages (or doctors), others manage to satisfactorily manipulate these authority systems to their own advantage. One such woman was Yalta, whom we met in the chapter on virtue and power in society. Yalta was to the manor born, so to speak. She was the daughter of the Exilarch, the secular ruler of the Jewish community in Babylonia (B. *Chullin* 124a; B. *Kiddushin* 70a), and so came from a powerful and prestigious family.

The position of Exilarch has no exact modern equivalent. The Jewish community in exile was administered by the Exilarch who was able to punish wrongdoers, appoint judges, and basically serve as governor of the community in administering its secular needs. As with any institution lasting as long as this one (the first twelve centuries C.E.), the Exilarch's power and duties varied with historical circumstances.

Yalta, as an Exilarch's daughter, was apparently used to receiving satisfaction from the sages: she recognized their authority but did not see them as all-powerful. She seems to operate on the premise that women have authority of their own in these matters, and when they share their expertise with the sages, they may expect that the sages will listen to them.

> Yalta once brought some blood to Rabbah bar Bar Hana, who informed her that it was unclean. She then took it to Rav Isaac, the son of Rav Judah, who told her that it was clean. But how could he act in this manner, seeing that it was taught: "If a sage declared [aught] unclean another sage may not declare it clean; if he forbade anything his colleague may not permit it?" (B. *Chullin* 44b) At first he [Rav Isaac] informed her indeed that it was unclean [out of respect for Rabbah bar Bar Hana], but when she told him that on every other occasion he [Rabbah] declared such blood as clean, but that on the last occasion [when he declared it unclean] he had a pain in his eye, he [Rav Isaac] gave her his ruling that it was clean. But are women believed in such circumstances?—Yes, and so it was also taught: A woman is believed when she says, "I saw a kind of blood like this one but I have lost it." (B. *Niddah* 20b)

Yalta plays by the rules but is not overwhelmed, or overrun, by them. She brings a sample of blood to Rabbah bar Bar Hana, expecting a ruling, as in every previous case, that it was clean, that is, that it is not menstrual blood but is simply blood as might be emitted from a cut, which is not ritually impure. However, in this instance, he is having trouble with his eyes and misjudges the blood as unclean. Yalta is aware that this is an incorrect ruling and goes to R. Isaac to have it overturned. At first, R. Isaac is reluctant to overturn his colleague's ruling. However, when Yalta explains the situation, R. Isaac agrees with her and rules that the blood is clean. In the context of the *Gemara*, this story illustrates the point that women are believed when they state a precedent regarding such blood samples. This passage is only one of a long string of stories about sages judging the nature of impurities. Interestingly, most of these stories portray the sages as reluctant to engage in such evaluations.

A Disabled Woman Acts as an Expert

Male authorities could, apparently, be bypassed altogether, and we do have a record of women adjudicating cases of ritual purity without the sages' help, as in the following case from the *Bavli*. Before we read it, however, we need to know that *terumah*, a farmer's gift of produce to a priest, could only be eaten by the priest and his family when they were in a state of ritual purity. So a priest's wife would have to examine herself to make sure that she had no menstrual flow or other impure discharge before eating *terumah*. The question raised in this passage is, "Which women are competent to make such an examination?" A blind woman could obviously not make such an examination, since it involves sight. Likewise, the sages felt that mentally ill and mentally disabled women, as well as deaf-mute women, could not reliably make such an examination. Why? Because the former were deemed intellectually unable to make the examination. The latter were disqualified because this ruling was made in an age before systematic communication with congenitally deaf persons was developed. Therefore, the sages believed that a person who was born deaf was mentally incompetent. However, they were well aware that a person who had had hearing, had learned to talk and then, through disease or age lost their hearing, was completely rational and was able to communicate.

> *Mishnah*: In the case of a deaf-mute woman or a mentally disabled woman or a blind or an insane woman, if other women of sound senses are available they attend to her, and she may then eat *terumah*.
> *Gemara*: Why should not a deaf-mute woman make her own examination, seeing that it was taught: Rabbi stated, A deaf woman was living in our neighborhood and not only did she examine herself but her friends also on observing a discharge would show it to her? There it was a woman who could speak but not hear while here the reference is to one who can neither speak nor hear; as we have learned: The deaf person of whom the sages spoke is always one who can neither hear nor speak. (B. *Niddah* 13b)

The commentary to this mishnah in the *Bavli* wonders why a deaf woman could not make such an examination and then mentions that Rabbi knew a deaf woman (most likely a woman who had been able to hear earlier but who had grown deaf later in life) who not only made her own examination but also helped the women in her neighborhood to determine whether or not they were ritually pure. Here is a disabled woman functioning as

an authoritative expert and recognized as such by a famous sage!

The Sages Shared Their Authority
with Women

This passage, along with the others we have studied, suggests that in some areas of women's lives, particularly
pertaining to women's health, there may have been whole
domains that the sages allowed women to adjudicate for
themselves. The sages may have recognized women as
experts when it came to examining blood samples to
determine if they were menstrual blood or some other sort
of discharge and practices relating to pregnancy, childbirth, and nursing. In other words, *the sages shared authority with women in these areas.*

The passages we have presented in this section show
us a wide range of approaches to women's ritual purity.
In one case, the sage seems to have complete authority
to question a woman and render a decision. Then we have
a case wherein authority for such decisions appears to
be shared by women and the sages. Finally, we have a
case that suggests that some women may have bypassed
the sages altogether and sought out other women who
were authorities on this issue rather than sages. Now that
women are able to serve as rabbis and cantors, hopefully
this sort of private "women's knowledge" will become part
of Judaism's "public record." In any case, we find that
women then, as women now, varied widely in their approaches to Jewish law and the authorities whom they
consulted about it. And we find that the sages recognized

women's expertise and ability to adjudicate these questions for themselves or together with the sages.

Sexual Decorum

The sages apparently felt a great deal of ambivalence about sex and sexuality (who does not?). On the one hand, sexual intercourse was an activity to be engaged in with a maximum of restraint and decorum. The sages, like the Greeks and Romans of that era, believed that the way sexual intercourse was engaged in affected the kind of child that intercourse produced. Marital rape was thought to result in unworthy children, while loving relations were believed to produce meritorious children.

> Whoever compels his wife to the [marital] obligation will have unworthy children. . . . Each woman who solicits her husband to the [marital] obligation will have children the like of whom did not exist even in the generation of Moses. (B. *Eruvin* 100b)

The sages, and their wives, were thought to be role models in every way, including in terms of sexual intercourse. Thus, it is not surprising that we find a passage in which Imma Shalom, the wife of Rabbi Eliezer and the sister of Rabban Gamaliel, is consulted about the correct conduct of marital relations. She was not only a member of two wealthy, pious, and powerful families but, as we have seen, she was also extremely righteous and clever.

> Imma Shalom was asked: Why are your children so exceedingly beautiful? She said to them: Because he [my husband] "converses" with me neither at the beginning

nor at the end of the night, but [only] at midnight; and when he "converses," he uncovers a handbreadth and covers a handbreadth, and is as though he were compelled by a demon. And I said to him, "What is the reason for this [for choosing midnight]?" And he said to me, "So that I may not think of another woman [who can be seen at night and early in the morning] lest my children be as bastards." (B. *Nedarim* 20a–b)

It was assumed that Imma Shalom and Rabbi Eliezer had beautiful children because they conducted their sexual intercourse in the most proper way, as befit an eminent sage and a woman of high birth. The term "converse" is a euphemism for sexual intercourse. The proper time for intercourse, according to Rabbi Eliezer, is in the middle of the night, for he considered that if he was thinking of another woman while cohabiting with his wife any ensuing children would be the products of adultery, even if the adultery was only in his mind. Interestingly, the students ask Imma Shalom, not Rabbi Eliezer, these questions. Was she considered an equal or greater authority on these matters? Or could Rabbi Eliezer have been in a state of excommunication when these questions were asked, and so they could not be posed directly to him? This is a possibility since we know that Rabbi Eliezer was excommunicated by the sages.

Sexual intercourse was not considered a mere physical activity by the sages. It, and its outcomes, were intimately involved with one's morality and the amount of one's learning, which were also seen as interconnected. Because sexual intercourse can involve some blurring of the boundaries between persons and between male and female, and also the weakening or abandonment of the rational self, the sages felt it should be carried out in as decorous a manner as possible so that these chaotic forces would not destroy the order the sages were trying to bring to their world.

Rabbi Eleazar and Rabbi Jochanan Take on the Essence of Womanhood

On the other hand, the sages give evidence that they relished these basic conundrums of sexual contact and identity that could not be contained or denied by any amount of decorum. In fact, in our next, quite lengthy passage, it seems that some sages envied women and sought to become like them in their ability to embody both life and death. This passage is found in B. *Bava Metsia* 83b–84b and is quite complicated and can be comprehended on a multitude of levels. To understand this passage, we need some background information about Rabbi Eleazar, its protagonist, whose life, as we shall see, is marked by the bizarre. Rabbi Eleazar was a sage at the end of the second century c.e. Even as a boy, he lived in a bizarre way for a time due to the persecution by the government of his father, Rabbi Simeon bar Yochai. Rabbi Simeon had taught Torah when it was banned by Hadrian and so was forced to hide.

> He and his son went and hid themselves in the House of Study, [and] his wife brought them bread and a jug of water and they dined. When the decree [against Torah study] became more severe he said to his son, Women are of unstable temperament: She may be put to the torture and expose us. So they went and hid in a cave. A

miracle occurred and a carob tree and a water well were created for them. They would strip their garments and sit up to their necks in sand. The whole day they studied; when it was time for prayers they robed, covered themselves, prayed, and then put off their garments again, so that they should not wear out. Thus they dwelt twelve years in the cave. Then Elijah came and stood at the entrance to the cave and said, Who will inform the son of Yochai that the emperor is dead and his decree annulled? So they emerged. Seeing a man plowing and sowing, they said, "They forsake life eternal [Torah study] and engage in life temporal [farming]!" Whatever they cast their eyes upon was immediately burnt up. Thereupon a *Bat Kol* (a Heavenly Voice) came forth and said to them, "Have you emerged to destroy My world? Return to your cave!" So they returned and dwelt there twelve months, saying, "The punishment of the wicked in Gehenna is [limited to] twelve months." A *Bat Kol* then came forth and said, "Go forth from your cave!" Thus they issued: Wherever Rabbi Eleazar wounded, Rabbi Simeon healed. Said he to him, "My son! You and I are sufficient for the world [our Torah study suffices for the world and everyone else can farm]." (B. *Shabbat* 33b)

Even from his childhood, Rabbi Eleazar seems destined to a life characterized by the bizarre, in terms of his physical development. And what is the impetus for their hiding in the cave? It is Rabbi Simeon's lack of faith in his wife's ability to withstand suffering. So Rabbi Eleazar, with his father, retreats into a cave and is "reborn," as it were, in a new, more spiritually intense form. And we note that they are "reborn" without the help of women. Rabbi Simeon b. Yochai claims (B. *Sukkah* 45b) that his suffering, and his son's suffering, are so powerful that they can exempt

the whole world from judgment from its creation to the
time of his speaking.

We do not know very much about Rabbi Eleazar's
mother. Was she weak willed? Or was Rabbi Simeon over-
whelmingly strong in this regard and so anyone else would
appear weak? Or, perhaps, is this statement ironic or
envious? Was a woman's ability to stand suffering part
of the spiritual power that Rabbi Simeon and Rabbi
Eleazar wished to acquire? Women could bleed each
month in an uncontrolled way and yet not die as uncontrolled bleeding would cause in any other case. Women
could bear the pain of childbirth repeatedly and bring from
it new life: they could lose a part of themselves in a gen-
erative way. Could it be that Rabbi Eleazar was taking on
this ability that must have seemed mysterious and mystical and that seemed reserved only for women? This is a
possibility, given the rest of his story (B. *Bava Metsia*
83b–84b), which we will examine in segments.

> Rabbi Eleazar, son of Rabbi Simeon, once met an officer
> of the [Roman] government who had been sent to arrest
> thieves. He said to him, How can you detect them? Are
> they not compared to wild beasts, of whom it is written,
> "Therein [in the darkness] all the beasts of the forests
> creep forth" (Psalm 104:20). (Others say he referred him
> to the verse, "He lies in wait secretly as a lion in his den.
> [He lies in wait to catch the poor; he does catch the poor
> when he draws him up in his net" [Psalm 10:9].) Maybe,
> [he continued,] you take the innocent and allow the guilty
> to escape? He [the officer] said to him, "What shall I do?
> It is the king's command." Said the Rabbi, "I will teach
> you what to do. Go into a tavern at the fourth hour of the
> day [about 10:00 A.M.]. If you see a man dozing with a
> cup of wine in his hand, ask what he is. If he is a learned

man, [you may assume that] he has risen early to pursue his studies; if he is a day laborer he must have been up early to do his work; if his work is of the kind that is done at night, he might have been rolling thin metal. If he is none of these, he is a thief; arrest him." The report [of this conversation] was brought to the court, and they said: Let the reader of the letter become the messenger. Rabbi Eleazar, son of Rabbi Simeon, was accordingly sent for and he proceeded to arrest thieves. Thereupon Rabbi Joshua, son of Karhah, sent [word] to him, "Vinegar, son of wine! How long will you deliver up the people of our God for slaughter!" He sent [back the reply], "I weed out thorns from the vineyard." [Rabbi Joshua] sent [back], "Let the owner of the vineyard himself [God] come and weed out the thorns."

One day a fuller met him, and called him: "Vinegar, son of wine." Said [the rabbi to himself], "Since he is so insolent, he is certainly an evildoer." So he told them [his attendants]: "Arrest him! Arrest him!" When he regained his senses, he went after him in order to secure his release but did not succeed. [Thereupon], he applied to him [the fuller] the verse, "Whoso keeps his mouth and his tongue, keeps his soul from troubles" (Proverbs 21:23). Then they hanged him and he [Rabbi Eleazar, son of Rabbi Simeon] stood under the gallows and wept. Said they [his disciples] to him: "Rabbi, do not let this thing be evil in your eyes, for he and his son seduced a betrothed maiden on the Day of Atonement." [On hearing this,] he laid his hand upon his heart and exclaimed, "Rejoice my heart! If matters on which you [the heart] are doubtful are thus, how much more so those on which you are certain! I am well assured that neither worms nor decay have power over you." Yet in spite of this, his conscience disquieted him. Thereupon, he was given a sleeping draught, taken into a marble chamber, and had his abdomen opened, and basketsful of fat removed from him and placed in the sun during Tammuz and Av and yet it did not putrefy. But no fat putrefies! [True,] no fat putrefies; nevertheless, if it contains red streaks, it does. But here, though it contained red streaks, it did not. Thereupon he applied to himself the verse, "My flesh too shall dwell in safety" (Psalm 16:9). (B. *Bava Metsia* 83b)

This part of Rabbi Eleazar's story gives us essential background that we will need to understand that part of his story that involves the women in his life more directly. Given all he has suffered at the hands of the government before this, it is not surprising that he is guilt stricken at condemning someone else to suffer simply because he feels insulted. The fuller's insult touches on Rabbi Simeon's virtue and Rabbi Eleazar's relative lack of it: Rabbi Simeon is wine and his son is merely vinegar— derivative and sour. Rabbi Eleazar is consoled somewhat when he learns that this man, together with his son, violated a betrothed virgin on the Day of Atonement, thereby breaking about as many Jewish laws as possible with one act of intercourse and, in the process, meriting the death penalty several times over. However, to prove to himself, and perhaps others, that he is truly virtuous, Rabbi Eleazar has huge basketsful of fat removed from his body and placed in the sun in the middle of summer and the fat does not rot. Thus, his body is able to blur distinctions between life and death and the boundary between what is in and of his body, and what is not. These distinctions are blurred in women's bodies, as well, particularly with respect to menstrual blood and the blood of parturition. Likewise, a pregnant woman loses what appears to be a part of her body in the process of childbirth; so Rabbi Eleazar becomes like a woman in the most profound sense through this ordeal.

Rabbi Eleazar is also like a woman in that his belly is grotesquely huge, as is a pregnant woman's. The ability of a woman's uterus to dramatically swell to many times its usual size is echoed in Rabbi Eleazar's, and Rabbi Ishmael's, huge bellies and sexual organs.

> . . . When Rabbi Ishmael, son of Rabbi Jose, and Rabbi Eleazar, son of Rabbi Simeon, met, one could pass through with a yoke of oxen under them and not touch them. Said a certain matron to them, "Your children are not yours!" They said to her, "Theirs [our wives'] are greater than ours." "[But this proves my allegation] all the more!" [she observed]. Some say they said to her: "For as a man is, so is his strength" (Judges 8:21). Others say, they said to her thus: Love suppresses the flesh. But why should they have answered her at all; is it not written, "Answer not a fool according to his folly?" (Proverbs 26:4)—To permit no stigma on their children. . . . (B. *Bava Metsia* 84a)

Apparently, Rabbi Ishmael and Rabbi Eleazar had gargantuan stomachs (just like pregnant women). Looking at them, the matron cannot imagine how these men would manage to have sexual intercourse. However, the two sages assure the matron that their wives' sexual organs, or perhaps bellies, are even larger than their own. Imagining these two grotesquely obese pairs, the matron can imagine even less credibly that intercourse is possible. Yet, the two sages reply that their powers of procreation are as powerful as their size and so intercourse is feasible and they are, indeed, the father of their own children. In this passage, the men and women seem almost equal in their hugeness and fertility, although there is the recognition that the women are even greater in this regard than the men.

We might say a word about this matron. She could be a Jew or a non-Jew, and we do not know whether she studied Torah or not. What we do know is that she may be the ancestress of women who, to this day, nag the rabbi about his or her appearance and speculate about the rabbi's sex life.

Interjected into this material is yet another story in which the line between maleness and femaleness is blurred.

> Rabbi Jochanan used to go and sit at the gates of the *mikveh*. He said, "When the daughters of Israel ascend from the bath, let them look upon me, that they may bear children as beautiful and as learned as I." Said the rabbis to him, "Do you not fear an evil eye?" He said to them, "I am of the seed of Joseph, against whom an evil eye is powerless." For it is written, "Joseph is a fruitful bough, even a fruitful bough by a well (*alei ayin*)" (Genesis 49:22). And Rabbi Abahu said, "Do not read by a well (*alei ayin*) but rather above the power of the eye (*olei ayin*)." Rabbi Jose son of Rabbi Chanina deduced it from the following: "and let them multiply abundantly like fish in the midst of the earth (Genesis 48:16)": just as fish in the seas are covered by water and the eye has no power over them, so also are the seed of Joseph—the eye has no power over them. (B. *Bava Metsia* 84a)

What is going on here? Women go to the *mikveh* and, in the normal course of things, immediately return home and have sexual intercourse in the hopes of conceiving children. Rabbi Jochanan, sitting by the *mikveh*, spiritu-

ally contributes to this process of procreation by letting
the women contemplate his beauty and learning, thereby
making the children, in some ways, his own. The image
of a bough by a well is an obvious symbolic portrayal of
the procreative act. Rabbi Jose prefers to liken Rabbi
Jochanan's power in the community's procreation to the
more ambiguous and fertile image of the fish, whose
massive procreation through the release of myriad eggs
takes place in the water, just as the *mikveh*'s water is
instrumental in a woman's procreative cycle. There is one
other indication that Rabbi Jochanan's powers are not like
other men's: the eye is quite often a symbol of sexuality,
and the evil eye has no power over him. He participates
in procreation, but not through sexual intercourse. The
explanation of his immunity to the evil eye comes in the
form of a pun made by reading Genesis 49:22 in a slightly
different way from which it is written.

One way sages could create progeny without intercourse was through the raising up of disciples, as we see
in a further passage about Rabbi Jochanan:

> One day Rabbi Jochanan was bathing in the Jordan,
> when Reish Lakish saw him and leapt into the Jordan
> after him. Said he [Rabbi Jochanan] to him, "Your
> strength should be for the Torah." He [Reish Lakish] said
> to him, "Your beauty should be for women." Said he
> [Rabbi Jochanan] to him [Reish Lakish], "If you will re-
> pent, I will give you my sister [in marriage], who is more
> beautiful than I." He undertook [to repent]; then he
> wished to return and collect his weapons, but could not.
> [Subsequently Rabbi Jochanan] taught him Bible and
> *Mishnah* and made him into a great man.
>
> One day there was a dispute in the schoolhouse [with
> respect to the following:] a sword, knife, dagger, spear,

handsaw, and scythe—at what stage [of their manufac-
ture] can they become unclean? When their manufacture is finished. And when is their manufacture finished?
Rabbi Jochanan ruled: When they are tempered in a fur-
nace. Reish Lakish maintained: When they have been fur-
bished in water. Said he [Rabbi Jochanan] to him [Reish
Lakish]: A robber understands his trade. Said he to him:
And wherewith have you benefited me; there [as a rob-
ber] I was called Master, and here I am called Master. He
said to him: I benefited you by bringing you under the
wings of the *Shekhinah*, he retorted. Rabbi Jochanan
[thereupon] felt himself deeply hurt, [as a result of which]
Reish Lakish fell ill. His sister [Rabbi Jochanan's, the wife
of Reish Lakish] came weeping and said to him: [Forgive
him] for the sake of my son. He said to her, "Leave your
fatherless children. I will preserve them alive" (Jeremiah
49:11). "For the sake of my widowhood [then]!" He said
to her: "And let your widows trust in me" (Jeremiah
49:11). Rabbi Shimon ben Lakish died, and Rabbi
Jochanan was plunged into deep grief. Said the rabbis,
"Who shall go to ease his mind?" Let Rabbi Eleazar ben
Pedat go, whose disquisitions are very subtle. So he went
and sat before him; and on every dictum uttered by Rabbi
Jochanan he [Rabbi Eleazar ben Pedat] said: There is a
teaching that supports you. He said, "Are you the son of
Lakisha? When I state a law, the son of Lakisha used to
raise twenty-four objections, to which I gave twenty-four
answers, which consequently led to a fuller comprehen-
sion of the law; while you say, 'A teaching has been taught
that supports you': do I not know myself that my dicta
are right?" Thus he went on rending his garments and
weeping, "Where are you, o son of Lakisha, where are
you, o son of Lakisha," and he cried thus until his mind
was turned. Thereupon the rabbis prayed for him, and
he died. (B. *Bava Metsia* 84a)

Rabbi Jochanan's great beauty is described as making him like a woman. (A more traditional explanation of this sentence is that his beauty makes him attractive to women.) The image is magnified by the fact that he is in water, as a woman is often portrayed as being in a *mikveh*. Reish Lakish apparently mistakes him for a woman, but Rabbi Jochanan reframes their relationship as one of a parent to a child: he makes Reish Lakish his student. (Making a student out of a person is frequently likened to being a parent in rabbinic literature.) However, when Reish Lakish rebels, Rabbi Jochanan's powers cause him to fall ill. (Parenthetically, we note that their argument over "implements" becoming "real" in either fire or water might symbolize the way sexuality is realized—through sexual intercourse or the *mikveh*.) The reference to Reish Lakish's being a "robber" is due to his previous career as a gladiator. In that profession, one would obviously know all about the manufacture of weapons described in this passage. Reish Lakish attempts patricide by disagreeing with his "father's" teachings and so is killed off by that father. Once Rabbi Yochanan has committed the deed, however, he cannot be consoled and, mourning for his "son," he dies.

What role does Rabbi Jochanan's sister play in this story? She seems to play the role of Rabbi Jochanan's daughter and wife more than his sister. He is the "father" of her husband and offers to be "father" to her children when it appears that Reish Lakish will die. It seems that he will also somehow relieve her widowhood, functioning as father, husband, and provider. Rabbi Jochanan's role in this story is ambiguous: he is the universal life-giving entity and yet overwhelms, hurts, and even kills those about him. Here we have, again, the double-edged image of woman: she nurtures life in her womb and from her breasts, yet she bleeds and thus embodies death.

Rabbi Eleazar's story, which now continues, also embodies this sort of ambiguity. Unlike a normal male body, his can bleed but live; die but not decay.

[Reverting to the story of Rabbi Eleazar, son of Rabbi Simeon] yet even so, Rabbi Eleazar, son of Rabbi Simeon's fears were not allayed and so he undertook sufferings [to repent for having turned thieves over to the authorities]. Every evening they spread sixty sheets for him, and every morning sixty basins of blood and discharge were removed from under him. In the mornings his wife prepared him sixty kinds of pap, which he ate, and then recovered. Yet his wife did not permit him to go to the schoolhouse, lest the rabbis discomfort him. Every evening he would exhort them [his sufferings], "Come my brethren and familiars!" while every morning he exclaimed, "Depart, you disturbers of my studies!" One day, his wife, hearing him, said to him, "You yourself bring them [the sufferings] upon you; you have [already] squandered the money of my father's house!" So she left him and returned to her paternal home.

[Then] there came sixty seamen who presented him with sixty slaves, bearing sixty purses. They prepared sixty kinds of pap for him, which he ate. One day she [his wife] said to her daughter, "Go and see how your father is faring now." She went [and on her arrival] her father said to her, "Go tell your mother that our [wealth] is greater than theirs [i.e., his father-in-law's house]. He then applied to himself the verse, "She is like the merchant's ships; she brings her food from afar" (Proverbs 31:14). He ate, drank, and recovered, and went to the schoolhouse [as his wife was not there to prevent him from doing so]. Sixty specimens of blood were brought before him, and he declared them all clean. But the rabbis objected, saying, "Is it possible that there was not [at least] one about which there was some doubt!" He said to them, "If it be as I [said, i.e., they are all pure], let them all be males; if not let there be one female among them." They were all males and were named "Eleazar" after him. . . .

On his deathbed he said to his wife: I know that the rabbis are angry with me and will not properly attend to me [at burial]. Let me lie in an upper chamber, and do you not be afraid of me. Rabbi Samuel bar Nachmani said: Rabbi Jonathan's mother told me that she was informed by the wife of Rabbi Eleazar, son of Rabbi Simeon: "I kept him lying in that upper chamber not less than eighteen or more than twenty-two years. Whenever I ascended there, I examined his hair, and [even] if a single hair had fallen out, the blood would well forth. One day, I saw a worm issue from his ear, whereat I was much grieved, but he appeared to me in my dream and told me it was nothing." ["This happened," he said,] "because I once heard a scholar insulted and did not protest, as I should have done." Whenever two people came before him [in a lawsuit], they stood near the door, each stated his case, and then a voice issued from that upper chamber, saying, "So and so, you are liable; so and so, you are free."

One day his wife was quarreling with a neighbor, when the latter [reviled her,] saying, "Let her be like her husband, who was not worthy of burial!" Said the rabbis, "When things have gone thus far, it is certainly not proper." Others say Rabbi Simeon b. Yochai appeared to them in a dream, and said to them: I have something amongst you that you refuse to bring to me. Then the rabbis went to attend to him [for burial], but the townspeople of Akhbaria did not let them, because during all the years that Rabbi Eleazar, son of Rabbi Simeon, slept in his upper chamber, no evil beast came to their town. But one day—it was the eve of the Day of Atonement—when they were busily occupied, the rabbis sent [word] to the townspeople of Biri, and they brought up his bier, and carried it to his father's vault, which they found encircled by a serpent. Said they to it, "O snake, o snake, open your mouth and let the son enter to his father." Thereupon it opened for them. Then Rabbi sent [messengers] to propose [to Rabbi Eleazar's] his wife. She sent back to him: Shall a utensil, in which holy food has been used, be used for profane purposes! There [in the Land of Israel] the proverb runs: Where the master hung up his weapons, there the shepherd hung up his wallet. He sent [back] word to her, "Granted that he outstripped me in learning, but who is my superior in good deeds?" She returned [word] to him, "That he outstripped you in learning, I did not know. But I do know [that he exceeded you] in [virtuous] practice, since he submitted himself to sufferings [for penance]." (B. *Bava Metsia* 84b)

Obviously, this section of our story functions on many levels. One way of getting a handle on it is to examine all the things that are quantified with the number sixty, numbered in the order they are mentioned but arranged here to bring out their symmetry.

1. sheets under Rabbi Eleazar   9. boys named Eleazar
2. basins of blood   8. specimens of blood
3. kinds of pap   7. kinds of pap
4. seamen   6. purses
5. slaves

The equivalence of numbers 1 and 9, 2 and 8, and 3 and 7 is clear. Just as sheets may be used to catch a baby and the placenta and blood associated with it, sheets are laid under Rabbi Eleazar to catch the blood and discharge that emerged from him. Rabbi Eleazar emits sixty basins of blood just as the women bring sixty specimens of blood. Numbers 4, 5, and 6 could form a group symbolic of womanhood (water, servitude, and a "purse" that could symbolize the uterus or vagina). Note that these three factors, the seamen, slaves, and purses, only appear once Rabbi Eleazar's wife has left, perhaps replacing her in the logic of the story. Rabbi Eleazar in this story bleeds like a woman, has a sheet placed under him (like a woman about to give birth or like a menstruating woman?), and, through his correct interpretation of Jewish law, reincarnates himself by contributing to sixty acts of procreation. His suffering, not being buried after his death, and not decaying in this state, is thought to protect those around him from harm. This may be related to the way a womb protects a fetus and also to the way a fetus' condition resembles death (existing in darkness, being incommunicado, and yet not decaying) and thus the way a pregnant woman embodies life and death at the same time. Rabbi Eleazar's story ends when he rejoins his father in a cave, this time a burial vault, reminiscent of the years they spent together in a cave in his boyhood.

And what of Rabbi Eleazar's wife and daughter? Rabbi Eleazar's wife strikes one as eminently reasonable. She is irritated with Rabbi Eleazar for bringing these sufferings on himself and impoverishing her whole family and leaves him. This is possibly an example of a male/female role reversal. As men may be irritated or unsympathetic to a woman's monthly suffering or the complaints of pregnancy, so Rabbi Eleazar's wife has little patience with Rabbi Eleazar. She leaves, but, after sending her daughter to find out about Rabbi Eleazar, returns and preserves him in a state of undecaying death for many years, during which he guards the town from evil and continues to offer halakhic judgments from the grave. As the coda of the story, she rejects Rabbi Eleazar's rival, Rabbi, as a husband. She cites Rabbi Eleazar's incredible, voluntary suffering as a sign that he is a greater man than Rabbi and that Rabbi is not worthy of marrying her. Perhaps Rabbi Eleazar's wife, having lived through all the upheaval connected with Rabbi Eleazar's life, did not want to live with *any* man again.

There may be yet another layer of meaning to the gargantuan, male–female body of Rabbi Eleazar. The very first human being, Adam, was believed by the sages to be hermaphrodite, i.e., possessing sexual characteristics of both genders. In addition, this Adam was enormous. Before Adam sinned in the Garden of Eden, he was of massive height and extended from one end of the world to the other (*Genesis Rabbah* 19:9 and 21:3), and after the sin, his height was diminished until he reached only one hundred cubits, or about 210 feet in height (*Genesis Rabbah* 12:6). (There are alternative versions of this teaching that claim his height was as high as nine hundred cubits!) Rabbi Eleazar shares many of this mystical, primordial Adam's characteristics. He was (spiritually) "born" in earth (the cave), as Adam was. His body is huge, as Adam's was. He has male and female characteristics, as the first Adam was said to have had (*Leviticus Rabbah* 14:1). He sins and suffers as Adam did.

There is obviously a great deal going on here that could use serious, scholarly analysis. Could it be that Rabbi Eleazar's story has been shaped by the historical forces of its time and by ancient literary paradigms? Could it be that the symbols in this story hearken back to primordial humanity's eternal dilemmas: its original form that was little less than the angels; its androgyny; its sin, subsequent suffering, and atonement; its death that is a doorway to eternal life? It appears that Rabbi Eleazar's story may have been shaped to echo these ancient themes. Certainly, the Jewish people was recreating itself ex nihilo, as it were, in this era of history. Perhaps Rabbi Eleazar's character is shaped here to make him the new "Adam" of the Jewish people in a new (and hostile) world.

Women play an integral role in this whole, complicated passage. It appears that the sages in this passage envy women's abilities and constitutions and attempt to adopt womanly characteristics. Women are ambiguous, perhaps dangerous. They suffer, but they live. They bleed, but they survive. They give life, but they seem to embody death. Women are mysterious and powerful. Women are "other," yet certain extraordinary men can become that "other" by making their bodies boundaryless and by taking on suffering that brings life. So, in the end, women and men can be like each other in the epitome of personhood and the ability to foster future generations.

What can we learn from this story? First, we should note that the interpretation given here is but one among many (see the Bibliography for others) and that not everyone would agree with the meanings attributed to the tale here. Second, the processes of sex, menstruation, birth, and nursing bring up profound psychological and personal issues in both men and women. Men may find themselves jealous of their pregnant wives and wish they could experience such closeness with their unborn children. Women may find themselves reexamining their relationships with their parents as they mature sexually and have children of their own. Hidden memories may play powerful roles in one's attitudes toward sexuality and childbearing and child rearing. In a sense, these processes render every individual male and female child and adult at the same time, just as Rabbi Eleazar embodied the male and the female and the living and the dead at the same time. Perhaps the only thing we can say definitively is that when we really experience sexuality and fertility we are fully human—not merely male or female, adult or child. We are all of these at the same time. Women and men may envy one another and deal with that envy by incorporating the experience of the "other" into themselves. By experiencing every facet of our human nature, we can thereby come closer to knowing all that God has given to every human soul.

9

Women and Loss: Role versus Reality

How often do women, and men, feel tension when the roles they are assigned by society are at odds with the roles they wish to play in life? Lab scientists forced to be housewives. Fathers forced to go to an office every day. When we are assigned roles, if they do not fit our souls, we need not follow the dictates of society. This becomes clear when we contrast the way women were expected to deal with loss and death and the way they are reported to have dealt with these traumas.

A Woman's Role in Mourning

Women are assigned the role of emoting over death by the *Mishnah*. They are to express themselves with intense displays of ritualized mourning.

> On the first days of the months, on Chanukah and on Purim, women lament and beat their hands. But during neither one nor the other may they wail. The dead having been buried, they may neither lament nor beat their hands. What is lamentation? When they all lament as one. [What is] wailing? When one speaks and they all answer after her, for it is said, "And teach your daughters wailing, and a woman her neighbor lamentation" (Jeremiah 9:19). But in the future to come it says, "He will swallow up death forever and the Eternal, O God, will wipe away tears from all faces . . ." (Isaiah 25:8). (M. *Mo'ed Katan* 3:9)

This mishnah, the last in the tractate, describes how women were to mourn. They were to express themselves physically and vocally. The *Bavli* (B. *Mo'ed Katan* 28b) on this passage provides us with some of the songs women were reported to have sung as part of their lamentations.

When we begin to examine stories of how women actually mourned and dealt with death, we must sound a note of caution. All of them are shaped into legends designed to underscore the universal values that we saw the sages expounding in our previous chapters: Torah transcends gender, virtue is the source of power, women can pronounce truth as readily as men. Mourning, the sages tacitly admit, is a human phenomenon, not a male or female one. These stories may have been selected to be the basis for legends because they are remarkable. In every age, perhaps, it is what is exceptional that is recorded and retold time and again.

Martha

We begin with the story of Martha's demise. That rich widow approaches death as she approached life: from a

vantage point of power and privilege. She is not emotion-
ally distraught but rather attempting to manipulate her
situation to the very end. However, since one of the major
principles the sages attempt to bring forth in rabbinic literature is that virtue, not money, is the source of power,
they portray Martha's death in a way that underscores this
point.

> The *biryoni* [Zealot bands] were then in the city. The
> rabbis said to them: Let us go out and make peace with
> them [the Romans]. They would not let them, but on the
> contrary said, Let us go out and fight them. The rabbis
> said: You will not succeed. They then rose up and burned
> the stores of wheat and barley so that a famine ensued.
> Martha the daughter of Boethus was one of the richest
> women in Jerusalem. She sent her manservant out say-
> ing, Go and bring me some fine flour. By the time he went,
> it was sold out. He came and told her, There is no fine
> flour, but there is white [flour]. She then said to him, Go
> and bring me some. By the time he went the white flour
> had sold out. He came and told her, There is no white
> flour, but there is dark [flour]. She then said to him, Go
> and bring me some. By the time he went the dark flour
> had sold out. He came and told her, There is no dark flour,
> but there is barley [flour]. She then said to him, Go and
> bring me some. By the time he went the barley flour had
> sold out. She had taken off her shoes, but she said, I will
> go out and see if I can find anything to eat. Some dung
> stuck to her foot and she died. Rabban Yochanan
> b. Zakkai applied to her the verse, "The tender and deli-
> cate woman among you who would not adventure to set
> the sole of her foot upon the ground" (Deuteronomy
> 28:56).
> There are those who say that she ate a fig left by
> R. Zadok and became sick and died. For R. Zadok ob-
> served fasts for forty years in order that Jerusalem might

not be destroyed [and became so thin that] when he ate anything the food could be seen [as it passed through his throat]. When he wanted to restore himself, they used to bring him a fig, and he used to suck the juice and throw the rest away.

When Martha was about to die, she brought out all her gold and silver and threw it in the street, saying, "What is the good of this to me?" and thus it is written, "They shall cast their silver in the streets" (Ezekiel 7:19). (B. *Gittin* 56a)

First we note that this entire story is told in Aramaic, meaning it is probably later rather than earlier in composition, and therefore relatively far removed in time from the events it describes that would have taken place in 70 C.E. And of course, the symmetry and logical progression of the famine's course as well as the neat illustrations of biblical verses that the story provides are all indications that this is a fable and not an actual episode from Martha's life, although she may indeed have been impoverished by the siege against Jerusalem.

Only a few things in this passage need explanation. The context for the verse from Deuteronomy is the long series of curses that are to befall the Jewish people if they break their covenant with God. Among them is the following, which was applied to Martha:

The tender and delicate woman among you, who would not venture to set the sole of her foot upon the ground for fastidiousness and delicateness, her eye shall be evil toward the husband of her bosom, and toward her son and toward her daughter and toward her afterbirth that comes out from between her legs, and toward her children whom she shall bear; for she shall eat them for want of all things in secret; because of the siege and distress, wherewith your enemy shall distress you in your gates. (Deuteronomy 28:56–57)

Similarly, Ezekiel the prophet predicts a time when a siege will bring rich and poor together in a state of poverty, hunger, and terror:

They shall cast their silver in the streets, and their gold shall be like an unclean thing: their silver and their gold shall not be able to deliver them in the day of the wrath of the Lord: they shall not satisfy their souls, neither fill their bowels because it is the stumbling block of their iniquity. (Ezekiel 7:19)

The whole story of Martha's death is shaped to underscore the sages' basic values: money could not save even the wealthiest and most influential of persons from starvation and disaster. Martha finally realizes this when she rejects her money as she faces death. This story illustrates a fine point: women are just as capable of being materialistic as men. Often, the only time when people who are trapped in greed and a desire for things can free themselves is when they face death and realize how worthless money is when they face their own mortality. This lesson may be especially hard for those who exercised great power in life to learn that all earthly power, except the power derived from virtue, must be abandoned at the grave.

Even though this is a legend, what we see is a woman who, far from being overcome by emotion, is coldly rational during a tumultuous time in history. She will do what she can to survive and when survival is no longer possible, she consciously faces death with steadfastness.

Martha could well be the foremother of those heroic women who, during the Holocaust and the building of the State of Israel, used their money and their courage to subvert death and sustain life, not only for themselves but also for others unknown to them.

Beruriah

If Martha faced death armed with the resource of money, Beruriah faced death with her greatest resource: her intellect. The four legends about Beruriah's ability to cope with loss that we find in rabbinic literature also serve to underscore the sages' value system. In each of them, she shows a mastery of text that transcends her gender and an ability to recognize virtue, and Torah learning, as the only true source of power. For example, at her brother's funeral Beruriah is able, like her father and mother, to give him a eulogy befitting his character. We have two versions of this text. The one from *Lamentations Rabbah* (a work probably composed in the first half of the fifth century C.E.) is probably the earlier one. Why? Because it seems to have been composed specifically to explain the following verse from Lamentations: "He has also broken my teeth with gravel stones. He has made me to wallow in ashes" (Lamentations 3:16). What specific series of events could cause someone's mouth to be filled with gravel and then covered in ashes? This story provides the answer.

> "He has also broken my teeth with gravel stones" (Lamentations 3:16). It is related of the son of R. Hananya b. Teradion that he became friends with robbers whose secret he disclosed, so they killed him and filled his mouth

with dust and pebbles. After three days they placed him in a coffin and wished to praise [i.e., pronounce a eulogy] over him out of respect for his father, but he [R. Hananya b. Teradion] would not permit them to do so. He said to them, "Allow me and I will speak concerning my son." He opened [his discourse] and said, "Neither have I hearkened to the voice of my teachers, nor inclined my ear to them that instructed me! I was well nigh in all evil in the midst of the congregation and assembly" (Proverbs 5:13–14). And his mother recited over him, "A foolish son is the vexation to his father, and bitterness to her that bore him" (Proverbs 17:25). His sister recited over him, "Bread of falsehood is sweet to a man; but afterward his mouth shall be filled with gravel" (Proverbs 20:17). (*Lamentations Rabbah* 3:15 ¶ 6)

Notice how symmetrically this midrash is composed: it begins with a verse about gravel in the mouth and ends with one. Here, R. Hananya b. Teradion, his wife, and his daughter Beruriah refuse to even allow a eulogy to be given for their son and brother. They do not hesitate to display their knowledge (and note that Beruriah's mother recites her own verse) and condemn their kin, who has not lived up to the family's standards of morality and scholarship. In this context, it is quite logical that Beruriah's brother's mouth is filled with gravel since he offended the robbers with his mouth.

Our other version of this text is found in tractate *Semachot*, which outlines the laws of mourning. The tractate is dated anywhere from the end of the third century to the eighth century, and here the passage seems to have been adapted to apply to the topic under discussion, which is how much of a corpse must be present in order to bring the dead out on a bier.

It is related of the son of R. Hananya ben Teradion that he took to evil ways and robbers seized and killed him. After three days his swollen body was found; they placed him in a coffin, set him on a bier, took him into the city and paid him a eulogy out of respect for his father and his mother. His father quoted over him the verse, "And you moan, when your end comes, when your flesh and your body are consumed, and say, 'How have I hated instruction, and my heart despised reproof; neither have I hearkened to the voice of my teachers, nor inclined my ear to them that instructed me! I was well nigh in all evil in the midst of the congregation and assembly'" (Proverbs 5:11–14). When he had finished he went back to the beginning of the verse. His mother quoted over him the verse, "A foolish son is the vexation to his father, and bitterness to her that bore him" (Proverbs 17:25). His sister quoted over him the verse, "Bread of falsehood is sweet to a man; but afterward his mouth shall be filled with gravel" (Proverbs 20:17). (*Semachot* 12:13)

Note that here, R. Hananya b. Teradion does allow a eulogy to be given for his son, whereas in our previous text this was not the case. Also, Beruriah's choice of a verse seems less appropriate here than in our first version, perhaps suggesting that the text in *Lamentations Rabbah* is the earlier one. In both cases, Beruriah and her mother seem to be equal participants in giving the eulogy with R. Hananya. They share his role in mourning rather than taking on the role prescribed for them by the *Mishnah*, emoting vigorously. Rather, they mourn by expressing themselves through Scripture.

When her father is martyred, Beruriah is able once more to cope with the great loss by using Torah knowledge to help her deal with her grief.

They then brought up Rabbi Hananya ben Teradion and said to him, "Why have you occupied yourself with Torah [forbidden by Hadrian under penalty of death]?" He said to them: "Thus the Lord my God commanded me." At once they sentenced him to be burned, his wife to be slain, and his daughter to be consigned to a brothel. . . . [As the three of them went out from the tribunal] they declared their submission to [the divine] righteous judgment. He said: "The Rock, His work is perfect; for all His ways are justice" (Deuteronomy 32:4). His wife said: "A God of faithfulness and without iniquity, just and right is He" (Deuteronomy 32:4). And his daughter said: "Great in counsel and mighty in work, whose eyes are open upon all the ways of the sons of men, to give everyone according to his ways, and according to the fruit of his doing" (Jeremiah 32:19). . . . They found Rabbi Hananya ben Teradion sitting and occupying himself with the Torah, publicly gathering assemblies and keeping a Scroll of the Law in his bosom. Straightaway they took hold of him, wrapped him in the Scroll of the Law, placed bundles of branches round him, and set them on fire. They then brought tufts of wool, which they had soaked in water, and placed them over his heart, so that his soul should not depart quickly. His daughter said to him, "Father, that I should see you in this state!" He said to her, "If it were I alone being burned it would have been a thing hard to bear; but now that I am burning together with the Scroll of the Law, He who will have regard for the plight of the Torah will also have regard for my plight." They [his disciples] said to him, "Rabbi, what do you see?" He said to them, "The parchments are being burned but the letters are soaring on high." "Open then your mouth" [said they] "so that the fire enter into you." He said to them, "Let Him who gave me [my soul] take it away, but no one should injure himself." The Executioner said to him,

"Rabbi, if I raise the flame and take away the tufts of wool from over your heart, will you cause me to enter into the life to come?" He said to him, "Yes." He said to him, "Then swear unto me." He swore unto him. He immediately raised the flame and removed the tufts of wool from over his heart, and his soul departed speedily. The Executioner then jumped and threw himself into the fire. And a *Bat Kol* came forth and said: "Rabbi Hananya ben Teradion and the Executioner have been assigned to the world to come." When Rabbi heard it he wept and said: "One may acquire eternal life in a single hour, another after many years." (B. *Avodah Zarah* 17b–18a)

Rabbi Hananya was one of the ten martyrs of the Hadrianic era who died with Rabbi Akiba. (We read their story on Yom Kippur.) The technique of putting water-soaked tufts of wool over the heart meant that the heart remained cool and continued beating while the rest of the body burned, producing the maximum amount of suffering. Whether the daughter of Rabbi Hananya ben Teradion in this story was Beruriah or a different daughter is a matter of dispute. Both Beruriah and her mother are once more portrayed as dealing with suffering through devotion to Torah, just as their husband and father does. In other words, the skills and attitudes needed to deal with adversity are not bound by gender roles.

Indeed, in the following passage, wherein Beruriah copes with the death of her two children, it is she, and not her husband, Rabbi Meir, who is able to use her knowledge of Jewish law to most effectively experience and guide the mourning process. It is from the Midrash on Proverbs, which is a late work (between the late eighth and late tenth centuries).

Another interpretation: "What a rare find is a capable wife" (Proverbs 31:10). A tale is told of Rabbi Meir that while he was sitting and expounding in the Academy on a Sabbah afternoon his two sons died. What did their mother do? She left them both lying on their couch and spread a sheet over them.

At the close of the Sabbath, Rabbi Meir came home from the Academy and asked her, "Where are my two sons?"

She replied, "They went to the Academy."

He said, "I looked for them at the Academy but did not see them."

She [silently] handed him the cup [of wine] for the Havdalah benediction, and he pronounced it. Then he asked her again, "Where are my two sons?"

She replied, "Sometimes they go someplace (maqom) [first]; they will be back presently." She served him [his meal] and he ate. After he recited the grace after meals she said to him, "Master, I have a question to ask you."

He replied, "Ask your question."

She said, "Master, some time ago a certain man came by and left something on deposit with me. Now he has come to reclaim this deposit. Shall I return it to him or not?"

He replied, "My daughter, is not one who holds a deposit obligated to return it to its owner?"

She said, "Without your opinion [on the matter] I would not give it back to him."

What did she do [then]? She took him by the hand, led him up to the children's room, brought him to the bed, and removed the sheet, so that Rabbi Meir saw them both lying on the bed dead. He burst into tears, saying, "My sons, my sons! My masters, my masters! My natural born sons, and my masters who enlightened me with their [learning in] Torah."

At this point Rabbi Meir's wife said to him, "Master, did you not just now tell me that we must return a pledge to its owner?"

To which he replied, "The Lord has given, and the Lord has taken away; blessed be the name of the Lord" (Job 1:21). R. Hananya said: In this manner she comforted him and brought him solace, hence it is said, "What a rare find is a capable wife!" (Proverbs 31:10). (*Midrash Mishlei,* chapter 31 on Proverbs 31:10)

To comprehend this story, we must understand some laws of mourning. One is not allowed to mourn on the Sabbath, and this is why Beruriah refrains from notifying her husband of their sons' deaths. Then, instead of telling him directly, she gives him a way of comprehending and dealing with his grief. She poses a legal question to Rabbi Meir, whose answer is obvious: when someone lends us valuables we must return them when asked to do so. Thus, she guides Rabbi Meir's grief. We have no record of *her* suffering, however. She apparently takes the role of "the strong one" in her family. Beruriah does quite the opposite of the ritualized mourning mandated for women by the Mishnah. Instead, she takes an almost intellectual approach to her mourning.

In families today, as well, women may be family leaders even when that position is nominally given to another family member. Women in our society are, more often than men, the ones who bear the inevitable price of a long and happy marriage: one partner will be left to mourn after the other is gone. And while expressing emotion is one essential part of the mourning process, we may take Beruriah as an example of a woman who used her intellectual gifts to help her deal with her grief.

Rabbi's Maid

Rabbi's maid is another woman who is portrayed as having the strength to deal with loss. While those about her wish to deny death's power, she is able to recognize when the time has come to let go of life.

> On the day Rabbi died the rabbis decreed a [public] fast and offered prayers for heavenly mercy. . . . Rabbi's handmaid ascended the roof and said: "The angels want Rabbi to join them and the people want Rabbi to stay with them. May it be the will [of God] that the people may overpower the angels." [However,] when she saw how often he resorted to the privy, painfully taking off his *tefillin* and putting them on again, she said, "May it be the will [of the Almighty] that the angels may overpower the people." As the rabbis incessantly continued their prayers for heavenly mercy, she took up a jar and threw it down from the roof to the ground. [For a moment] they stopped praying, and the soul of Rabbi departed to its [eternal] rest. (B. *Ketubot* 104a)

Rabbi's maid, like the sages, initially prays that Rabbi not die. But when she sees how painful life has become for him (it is forbidden to wear *tefillin*, which contain passages from Scriptures, into an outhouse) she prays that Rabbi may be allowed to die. Realizing that as long as the sages continued praying, Rabbi would not be allowed to die, since the tug-of-war between the sages and the angels was equally balanced, she broke a jar, which startled the sages into ceasing their prayers for a moment. So Rabbi was able to die and find peace. Here, Rabbi's maid's compassion and common sense overcome the prayers and emotions of the sages. And, we note, it is the (male) sages who are praying incessantly and with great emotion, not the lone woman in the story. She is the one who responds rationally and physically to the dilemma of Rabbi's demise.

Martha, Beruriah, and Rabbi's maid are portrayed as coping with grief with those resources they had in greatest abundance: money, knowledge of Torah, and righteousness rather than through overt emotional displays as mandated by the *Mishnah*. They found their own ways to transform suffering into acceptance and meaninglessness into meaningfulness. They are women who rejected the roles theoretically assigned to them and, instead, used all the gifts God gave them to fulfill their destiny. In such a way they, and we, can find fullness and peace.

Notes

Introduction

1. Bernadette J. Brooten, *Women Leaders in the Ancient Synagogue* (Atlanta: Scholars Press, 1982).

2. Jacob Neusner, *A History of the Jews in Babylonia,* vol. 5 (Leiden: E. J. Brill, 1970), pp. 329–342.

3. Erwin R. Goodenough, *Jewish Symbols in the Greco-Roman Period,* ed. and abr. Jacob Neusner (Princeton, NJ: Princeton University Press, 1992), p. 35.

Chapter 1: Torah Transcends Gender: Women and Sages' Learning

1. Adin Steinsaltz, *Tractate Bava Metsia,* vol. 1 of *Talmud Bavli* (Jerusalem: Israel Institute for Talmudic Publications, 1983), 59a, p. 247. The picture is also in Adin Steinsaltz, *The Talmud: The Steinsaltz Edition,* vol. 3, *Tractate Bava Metzia, Part III* (New York: Random House, 1990), p. 235.

2. Adin Steinsaltz, *Tractate Eruvin*, vol. 2 of *Talmud Bavli* (Jerusalem: Israel Institute for Talmudic Publications, 1982), 101b, p. 449.

Chapter 2: The Matron: Jew or Non-Jew?

1. Jacob Neusner, *The Midrash: An Introduction* (Northvale, NJ: Jason Aronson Inc., 1990), pp. 141–170.

Chapter 5: Virtue as Power II: Women and Power in Society

1. Susan Weidman Schneider, "Feminist Philanthropy: Women Changing the World with Their Dollars," *Lilith* 18:4 (Fall 1993): 14–17.

2. H. H. Sasson, *A History of the Jewish People* (Cambridge: Harvard University Press, 1976), p. 269. (Based on Josephus, *Antiquities*, Book 20, paragraph 54.)

Chapter 7: Diffidence and Distance: The Sages and Childbirth, Nursing, and Motherhood

1. Susan Starr Sered, *Women as Ritual Experts* (New York: Oxford University Press, 1992).

Bibliography

Adler, Rachel. "The Virgin in the Brothel and Other Anomalies: Character and Context in the Legend of Beruriah." *Tikkun* 3:6 (November/December 1988): 28–32 and 102–105.

    An interesting, readable examination of the stories in rabbinic literature concerning Beruriah.

Baskin, Judith R., ed. *Jewish Women in Historical Perspective*. Detroit: Wayne State University Press, 1991.

    A collection of articles written from a scholarly perspective.

Blackman, Philip. *Mishnayoth*. Gateshead: Judaica Press, 1977.

Boyarin, Daniel. *Carnal Israel*. Berkeley: University of California Press, 1993.

    In this book Boyarin explores many of the same passages found in this work. It is fascinating but written on an extremely scholarly level and may be difficult for the lay reader to understand.

———. "The Great Fat Massacre: Sex, Death, and the Grotesque Body in the Talmud." In *People of the Body: Jews and Judaism from an Embodied Perspective*, ed. Howard Eilberg-Schwartz, pp. 69–100. Albany: SUNY Press, 1992.

A scholarly, in-depth consideration of the story of Rabbi Eleazar. It is quite interesting but written on a very elevated level.

Brooten, Bernadette J. *Women Leaders in the Ancient Synagogue*. Atlanta: Scholars Press, 1982.

A scholarly consideration of nonliterary evidence of women's participation in the ancient synagogue.

Brown, Peter. *The Body and Society: Men, Women and Sexual Renunciation in Early Christianity*. New York: Columbia University Press, 1988.

A scholarly but very readable examination of men's and women's sexual identities in the rabbinic era.

Carmell, Aryeh. *Aids to Talmud Study*. Jerusalem: Feldheim, 1971.

A valuable reference work for the beginning Talmud student.

Encyclopaedia Judaica. Jerusalem: Keter, 1972.

Epstein, Dr. I., ed. *The Babylonian Talmud*. London: Soncino, 1948.

Freedman, H., and Simon, Maurice, eds. *Midrash Rabbah*. London: Soncino, 1983.

Friedman, Shamma. "Literary Development and Historicity in the Aggadic Narrative of the Babylonian Talmud—A Study Based Upon B.M. 83b–86a." In *Community and Culture: Essays in Jewish Studies in Honor of the Ninetieth Anniversary of the Founding of Gratz College*, ed. Nahum M. Waldman, pp. 67–80. Philadelphia: Gratz College Seth Press, 1987.

Another scholarly exploration of Rabbi Eleazar's story.

Goodenough, Erwin R. *Jewish Symbols in the Greco-Roman Period*, ed. and abr. Jacob Neusner. Princeton, NJ: Princeton University Press, 1992.

A marvelous book that puts the rabbinic era into its larger perspective. Fascinating and readable.

Hammer, Reuven. *Sifre: A Tannaitic Commentary on the Book of Deuteronomy*. New Haven: Yale University Press, 1986.

Hauptman, Judith. "Women's Liberation in the Talmudic Period: An Assessment." *Conservative Judaism* (Summer 1972): 22–28.

Henry, Sondra, and Taitz, Emily. *Written Out of History: Our Jewish Foremothers*. Sunnyside, NY: Biblio Press, 1988.
A popular work about little-known Jewish women throughout the ages.

Kalmin, Richard. "Talmudic Portrayals of Relationships between Rabbis: Amoraic or Pseudepigraphic?" *AJS Review* 17:2 (Fall 1992): 165–197.

Neusner, Jacob. *A History of the Jews in Babylonia*. 5 vols. Leiden: E. J. Brill, 1970.
This five-volume work provides an excellent introduction to the world the sages lived in. It is quite easy to read despite its length.

———. *The Midrash: An Introduction*. Northvale, NJ: Jason Aronson Inc., 1990.
A layperson's introduction to the Midrash collections.

———, ed. *The Talmud of the Land of Israel: A Preliminary Translation and Explanation*. 35 vols. Chicago: University of Chicago Press, 1984.

———, ed. *The Tosefta*. 6 vols. Hoboken: Ktav, 1986.

Romney Wegner, Judith. *Chattel or Person? The Status of Women in the Mishnah*. New York: Oxford University Press, 1988.
A scholarly work that explains why women are sometimes treated as property and other times as persons in rabbinic literature.

Sasson, H. H., ed. *A History of the Jewish People*. Cambridge: Harvard University Press, 1976.
A standard textbook of Jewish history.

Schneider, Susan Weidman. "Feminist Philanthropy: Women Changing the World with Their Dollars." *Lilith* 18:4 (Fall 1993): 14–17.

    An article that describes the way women's and men's philanthropy differ.

Sered, Susan Starr. *Women as Ritual Experts: The Religious Lives of Elderly Jewish Women in Jerusalem*. New York: Oxford University Press, 1992.

    A fascinating study of women's religious lives and the way they differ from men's. Quite readable.

Steinsaltz, Adin. *Talmud Bavli*. Jerusalem: Israel Institute for Talmudic Publications, 1983.

    The invaluable Hebrew translation of the Babylonian Talmud.

———. *The Talmud: The Steinsaltz Edition*. New York: Random House, 1989.

Visotzky, Burton L. *The Midrash on Proverbs: Translated from the Hebrew with an Introduction and Annotations*. New Haven: Yale University Press, 1992.

Index

About the Author

Judith Z. Abrams is a woman with a mission: she wants to bring the beauty of Talmud to as many people, and with as much depth, as possible. To that end, she has published three books on the Talmud (*The Talmud for Beginners*, volumes I and II, and with her husband, Dr. Steven A. Abrams, *Jewish Parenting: Rabbinic Insights*), earned her Ph.D. in rabbinic literature from the Baltimore Hebrew University, and teaches across the country. She is the founder and director of *Maqom*: A Place for the Spiritually Searching, a school for adult Talmud study where anyone can learn, regardless of their background. She lives in Houston with her husband, Steven, and their three children, Michael, Ruth, and Hannah.